To my children, Katherine Martin and
Charles Henry Lewis.
May they help to create an America of
fewer clients and victims . . .

American Politics in a Bureaucratic Age

Citizens, Constituents, Clients and Victims

Eugene Lewis

Hamilton College

Winthrop Publishers, Inc.
Cambridge, Massachusetts

Library of Congress Cataloging in Publication Data

Lewis, Eugene.
  American politics in a bureaucratic age.

  Includes bibliographical references and index.
    1. United States—Politics and government.
2. United States—Economic policy. 3. United
States—Social policy. 4. United States—Military
policy. 5. Bureaucracy. I. Title.
JK421.L48   353.01   77-1752
ISBN 0-87626-035-0
ISBN 0-87626-034-2 pbk.

Cover design by Hal Lewis Design, Inc.

© 1977 by Winthrop Publishers, Inc.
  17 Dunster Street, Cambridge, Massachusetts 02138

10 9 8 7 6 5 4 3 2 1

Contents

v

Preface

How is one to think about politics in a nation increasingly dominated by ubiquitous public and private bureaucracies? How might one conceive of citizenship, political participation, and representation in a setting of organizationally mysterious and mystified public policy processes? This book offers some partial answers to these questions. It does so through the integration of a series of participation concepts with a notion of public bureaucracy somewhat different from those typically found in the public administration literature. A theoretical structure is presented which deals with bureaucratic elaboration in terms of identified historical changes in political values. The focus of the analysis is generally directed at those points at which public bureaucracies interact with their environments. In this volume, organizations are construed as actors and emphasis is placed on internal characteristics deemed significant to policy-making processes. Important questions about the intraorganizational dynamics of political bureaucracies are not considered, although I plan to produce a companion volume that is concerned with these factors.

A standard conceit of books like this is the claim that they are suitable for students and specialists alike. I hope that I have achieved that favored mixture by attacking what I believe to be a major problem for political science and public administration in a fashion which will interest students while it provokes discussion among my fellow theorists. For this is a work of theory and a polemic as well, one that attempts to make some sense out of an aspect of American political life which has puzzled political scientists and politicians for at least three generations. In my treatment of this old question of bureaucracy in a democracy (to borrow Charles Hyneman's title), I have attempted to minimize the use of technical language and to provide reasonably familiar political and historical illustrations for my arguments.

A full introduction is presented in the first chapter of the book. Because this is the case, the usual prefatory remarks about the intent and scope of the work can be brief. This brevity allows me some space to tell what I believe to be a remarkable short story.

In the spring of 1975, I was the Provost of Hamilton College. While I enjoyed working in that peculiar vineyard known as academic administration, my thoughts often strayed to the ideas for this book. (It is axiomatic that administrators occasionally long for the "life" of faculty members, while the latter dream in the odd moment about the power, glory, and salary of the former.) During my career as a faculty member and later as a college bureaucrat, I met and came to know a remarkable man by the name of George Cogar who is a Trustee of Hamilton College and a widely respected innovator and entrepreneur in the computer world. Cogar and I had chatted about my ideas in a vague way over the years.

On a most unusual day in May, he casually inquired about my progress on this project. I admitted that I'd not gotten terribly far what with the "press of business" and the "burdens of administration." In the midst of this casual cliché-ridden conversation, Cogar announced that if I were willing he would donate to the College sufficient funds to support me over a three-year period. I was to do what I wanted with no strings attached. This was one of the few times in my life when no words came to my lips. Nor did they come to the lips of my friend and boss, J. Martin Carovano, President of Hamilton College, when first I told him about the offer and of my mixed feelings about leaving office. He understood that one simply could not turn down such an opportunity and accepted my resignation with regret, empathy, and grace. My short story ends with an expression of gratitude to Cogar and Carovano for their extraordinary generosity and kind understanding. I hope that this book goes part of the way toward justifying their confidence and good will.

Many people read and criticized some or all of this book in its several manuscript versions. Charles Levine of the Maxwell School of Syracuse University and R. P. Suttmeier of Hamilton College read the entire manuscript in earlier form. My colleagues at Hamilton and Kirkland College who read and often improved parts of the work include: Frank Anechiarico, John Bacheller, David Ellis, Donald Mead, Channing Richardson, Jeffrey Ross and Alphonse Sallett. Francis Rourke of Johns Hopkins and Thomas Cronin were helpful reviewers, and William J. Siffin of Indiana provided his usually pertinent stimulus.

My student assistant, Anne Rothwell, is the worthy successor in an unbroken line of intelligent and hardworking undergraduates who have helped with far more than the usual impedimentia of manuscript preparation. I have been blessed with students interested and capable enough to improve my work in a variety of ways. I thank them all and am delighted to recall my special debt to Lynn Appleton who was unaccountably deleted in my last preface.

Finally one must acknowledge that all contributions from others improved the text and that one's wife and children are to be thanked for enduring the behavioral irregularities said to be the result of writing books. I have no intention of ignoring these traditions and hereby admit that the parts of the book which the reader enjoys came from others while those bits which find less favor are solely my own. I am always a burden to my family and therefore have no specific apology to make.

Maren Donaldson Lewis is the hidden partner in this enterprise. She copyedited, typed, clarified, encouraged, and understood. I wish that I could have gotten her to write the book, but she insisted that she didn't know enough about the subject. Instead, she has agreed to accept whatever royalties are earned in partnership with those protean and lovable royalty-absorbers, Katie and Harry Lewis, to whom this book is dedicated.

E. L.
Clinton, N.Y.

chapter one

Public Bureaucracy
in Everyday Life

Introduction

I was brought up to believe that in America the people determined what the government is and does. Teachers, history books, friends, and the mass media led me to believe in the truth of certain propositions. I believed that through the electoral process, leaders gained high office in order to convert the will of the people into laws which were then faithfully executed by administrators. I was taught that candidacy equaled issue advocacy and that elected officials had the power, knowledge, and mandate to give the people the results they wanted. I believed that the government of the United States acted on the desires of the people through a set of historically sacred institutions and laws that guaranteed not only responsiveness, but also fairness, equity, and tolerance. Above all, I had an abiding faith in the heroic capacity of American governmental power to deal with any condition or crisis, domestic or foreign.

As I grew older, I became aware of "exceptions"[1] to these propositions and accounted for them in two ways. At first, I simply thought them aberrations—mistakes by honest men or the evil doings of evil men. Questions of right and wrong in politics could readily be resolved domestically by resort to political heroes and pronouncements. Foreign policy was easy: either "they" were on "our" side, or they were not. When

---

[1] This term comes from Murray Edelman, *The Symbolic Uses of Politics* (Urbana: University of Illinois Press, 1970). My introductory discussion parallels many of Edelman's analyses.

1

this first kind of explanation wore thin, I moved on to a second, more developmental rationale for the exceptions. I thought that they could be conceived of as "stumbling blocks" on the path toward realization of the propositions of my childhood that I had now come to believe were "ideals" rather than descriptive truth.

As my knowledge of the variety and magnitude of the exceptions grew, I began to suspect that they were not exceptions at all. The *expectations* of childhood belief mixed with the *exceptions* of emerging adult political knowledge led to inevitable clashes between myths and realities. There seemed to be forces in the world over which no one, apparently, had political control. I began to rethink my notions of politics and of the state itself. The symbols of sovereignty, of an heroic past and leadership, were no longer of much comfort. That common article of faith so present in my youth called "Americanism" or "believing in America" had little to do with my experience of America. The discrepancies between descriptions of politics and my observation of politics in a variety of settings left me with two very common feelings: moral outrage about the hypocrisy of it all and utter confusion about how things really worked. By the time I was twenty, I understood that the myths, symbols, and rituals of American democracy were, at least partially, devices to reassure and comfort the confused and uncertain.

The dramaturgical and psychoanalytic pronouncements of commentators and literary critics seemed as silly and irrelevant to me as the "inside dopesterism" of many journalists. Most of this conventional wisdom struck me as self-justifying and lacking in the kinds of connective or linkage wisdom I now sought. I now understood that there were relationships between politics, policy, and the conditions of the world around me, but I lacked a coherent explanation of those connections. Innocence knowing no bounds in recently awakened late adolescence, I determined to obtain some graduate degrees in political science. If I didn't resolve the dilemmas of primitive political consciousness, at least I might gain employment.

The need to be gainfully employed was a powerful and recurrent theme in my youth, as it was for everyone else I knew. One of the overwhelming lessons of that need was that it was most likely to be satisfied in an organizational setting. Everywhere I looked I discovered organizational requirements. Schooling, employment, even sociability and politics were enmeshed in organizations of one sort or another. A fact as obvious as the discontinuities between political mythologies and "exceptions" struck me: life in my country and in my time was taking place in organizationally defined or organizationally influenced contexts.

As simple-minded and obvious as these observations were, one more confronted me with equal force. I grew up in an era in which everything was understood to be in a state of change, development, or progress. This bit of conventional wisdom puzzled me, for I could not understand the place of the past in the rush of the present. Did it all disappear, or did some of it stay and shape what was going on, particularly in the political world?

I brought to my graduate training three unarticulated and vaguely related matters. How in fact might one think of the American political system such that one's description of it conformed in some way with at least some aspects of one's experience of it? What does the observation that we live in an organizational world have to do with government and politics? Finally, what is the relationship, if any, of the past to the present? I did not think of things as neatly as my questions might suggest. Rather, the questions had a tendency to arise episodically. Often I forgot them completely as I went about the business of being a graduate student, a public bureaucrat and, finally, a graduate student once again.

These years only strengthened my belief that an integrated notion of my three general questions was difficult to achieve. My years as a graduate student were valuable, however, for they taught me a concern for epistemology and the multiple meanings of theory and methodology. Confrontations with the thoughts of my living and dead intellectual betters also revealed some things about the history and sociology of knowledge.

American social science is as much an organizational phenomenon as anything else. Knowledge is organized into highly specialized fields of thinkers and expertise. My training, sensibly enough, required that I master the theory, methodology, technology, and substance of several subfields of political science. I learned that the several fields and subfields of social science had different stories to tell about my three questions. Each had a distinct set of approved methodological lenses through which to perceive political phenomena. Each had substantive emphases that concentrated on matters which varied greatly in the degree to which they were coincident with my three general concerns.

The limiting constraints of the various conceptual and methodological schools compounded these substantive divisions within the social sciences in general and in political science in particular. Although I discovered some shining, if not convincing exceptions, the general content of social science literature only embroidered the problem of integrating my three general questions.

In the fullness of time, I became a professor of political science and the question of an integrative notion of American politics was reopened for me in a most pressing manner. Students came to my classes in methodology, organization theory, and urban politics convinced that they had no problem in integrating American political phenomena. I was astounded to discover the repetition of the slogans and myths of my youth: the lyrics differed, but the melody lingered on. Given the chance to disassemble their tidy conceptual and emotional certainties about the political world and how one thinks of it, I happily did so. Occasionally, I succeeded in shaking their belief systems. Inevitably, there came a cry for me to put it all back together again the "right" way making sure that I included a reasonable dose of hope.

This I was unable to do to my satisfaction, so I turned to better minds and some more or less coherent schools of thought. Training, observation, reading, and limited participation led me back to the concerns of earlier years. This time I knew a little more about the discontinuities between disciplines, methodologies, and theories. Furthermore, I had sufficient hubris to believe that by integrating some of that knowledge, I could at least look at politics, policies, and government in a different way, which might lead toward synthesis and understanding.

Intellectual traditions that dealt with political power, organizational phenomena, and values as interrelated and vital aspects of an evolving American political system were difficult to find. But important statements about each were discoverable within the intellectual values of several disciplines.

My objective was to develop some concepts that would relate the behaviors of individuals and groups to a formulation of the ancient notion of the state. Consistent with this, I wished to explain some important aspects of political behavior in an historical and organizational context. The possibility of achieving so grand a goal was dim. It still is. But a realization of that goal seemed to me to lie in a work of integration that would attempt to tie together some of the thought possessed by the several disciplines.

This book, then, owes much to several traditions. In an important sense, it is a descendant of the public administration and democracy literature best exemplified in the modern era by the work of Dwight

Waldo, Emmette Redford, Frederick Mosher, Francis Rourke, and my late teacher Roscoe Martin. My groping with ways to understand the role of the past in the present is grounded in historians as diverse as Herbert Muller, Garrett Mattingly, Louis Hartz, and Richard Hofstadter. The insights into organizations provided by Herbert Simon, Chester Barnard, James D. Thompson, and my teachers Bertram Gross, Victor Thompson, and William Siffin were also vital to this undertaking.

The problem of integrating the work of these important thinkers is both aggravated and ameliorated by the general methodological and theoretical status of social science inquiry at the macroscopic level. The mechanical and organic theoretical metaphors which I believe dominate social science today are at once seductive and dangerous. The work of David Easton, Amitai Etzioni, and Karl Deutsch, among others, illuminates much of this book. As significant as structural–functional systems and communications theories are, I continue to have problems with the way they deal with problems of system boundary, requisite functions, equilibrium, change, history, and values. Although I adopt, reformulate, and ignore much of what these original thinkers say, I remain in their intellectual debt as the pages which follow clearly indicate.

Much valuable work of modern behavioral science has a tendency to deal with ever-smaller and more measurable aspects of political reality. The rigors of positivist methodology cause social scientists to confront those problems most amenable to their tools. While much of this book is, I believe, conducive to methodological reformulation, it will be a disappointment to those who comprehend politics and administration entirely on the grounds of available positivist and empirical technique.

The book will be disappointing in other ways. It fails to fully integrate the diverse phenomena of American politics in a bureaucratic age for two reasons. The first reason is understandable enough: the author lacks the insight and the knowledge to create a thoroughly consistent, integrated theory of American politics and bureaucracy. Of greater importance is the open question about the empirical reality of any fully integrated system. This book suggests that the phenomena studied are themselves unintegrated, unarticulated, and highly discontinuous. In other words, a political system, at least as we currently understand the notion of system, may not be in existence out there. Certainly, political life has systemic properties, but that does not mean that all significant structures, events, and actions are part of *a system*.

The pages that follow do not take into account all relevant factors.

They reflect in their disjointedness what I believe to be true of American politics in a bureaucratic age. The organization of the book reflects the goals I have set. These are:

1. To posit and explore the modes of interaction between citizens and public bureaucracy. I use the term "public bureaucracy" in its simplest meaning: formal organizations that act with the authority of the state.
2. To develop a conceptual framework that accounts for these modes of interaction over time.
3. To provide an analytic structure for describing the growth of bureaucratic political power.
4. To trace an evolving set of values, structures, and mechanisms (within defined realms of the political) which tend toward the development of a political system dominated by public bureaucracies and their constituent and clientele networks.

This chapter defines the modes of interaction (goal 1). Chapter two presents the conceptual framework (goals 2 and 3). Chapters three, four, and five deal with political economy, social welfare and control, and national defense (goal 4). Chapter six attempts to shed light on the interactive modes, some conceptions of public bureaucracy, and the role of professionalized bureaucrats in each political realm discussed.

Homo Bureaucratus

Most of us were born in hospitals at least parts of which were built and equipped by public funds administered by some public agency. The medical personnel who attended our births undoubtedly were educated from kindergarten through graduate school in institutions either wholly or partially supported and regulated by public agencies. Any medications were used only after they had received government approval as had the physician who prescribed them and the pharmacist who prepared them. Conditions of the delivery room and the certification that one has indeed been born are matters of direct governmental concern and regulation.

From birth to elementary school, the absence or presence of parents, their economic well-being, and indeed much of the simple surroundings of young children are affected in varying degrees by government involvement. The economic conditions which either enhance or detract from our parents' ability to support us are a function of governmental interventions through fiscal and monetary policies. Even the air we breathe and the water and food we consume are matters of direct state concern. Our lives are protected against violent biblical contingencies like fire, flood, and famine by public agencies.

For most of us education is a matter of the end products of public policy and management. What we learn, from whom we may learn it, and when we are supposed to learn are the legal responsibility of a set of public agencies. Within the public primary and secondary school, government agencies provide meals, dental services, eye examinations, and social service counseling for our families and ourselves should the need arise. Some services must be received on threat of legal sanction and others must be complied with under the duress of informal social sanction. American colleges and universities are increasingly dependent upon government funding and regulation, whether they are public institutions or not. Most of us attend public institutions of higher learning that are variously supported, regulated, and/or directed by some national, state, or local agency of government.

An enormous number of us enter a labor market dominated by public policy decisions and providing employment opportunities either in public bureaucracies themselves or in private firms whose economic well-being is directly related to the actions of government agencies. It is difficult to imagine many categories of employers unaffected by government policy as interpreted and implemented by public bureaucracies. Our personal income from employment is likely to be reduced by one-quarter to one-third as a result of taxation in one form or another. Our marriages, our home purchases, the threads of our adulthood from the liberation of the driver's license to the insurance of our burial . . . all of these major events in our individual biographies are regulated, limited, stimulated, or directly authorized by public agencies. Too often during the past thirty-five years millions of us have become actual or potential involuntary public employees of the armed forces.

As the beginning of our lives occurs under a variety of interventions from public agencies, so too are our later years likely to be heavily involved with such agencies. Once again we are probably hospital-bound. But this time we will undoubtedly have to stay a bit longer. The regulation, licensing, and whatnot of the services provided, while important, probably will not be paramount in our thoughts. Few of us can afford to pay for prolonged hospitalization and medical care if we are already dependent on government agencies to assist us in providing the necessities of everyday life. As our government-regulated pension plans are supplemented by the mandatory pension plan for which government has taxed us, we may begin to comprehend our growing dependence upon public bureaucracies for what is left of our lives.

Our biographies are molded by the actions of public organizations in an enormous and complex variety of circumstances. In nearly every instance mentioned above, *public organizations* intervene to expand or contract the possible courses of action open to us. An important series of questions seem to flow from these commonplace observations. How do we as citizens of a democratic society relate to these institutions of public control? In what ways are the policies, regulations, and "outcomes" of public organizations created? What have the traditional values of democracy like representation, accountability, and liberty itself to do with the operations of these organizations that are so crucial to the conduct of our everyday lives?

The view taken here is that rather than the *homo politicus*[2] archetype of Athens, our vision might be more accurately served by identifying the American public in terms of a *homo bureaucratus*, for in the important matters of our public lives we are more involved with public bureaucracy than we are with parties, elections, and legislatures. That element of American government and politics which consists of public organizations is an increasingly significant institutional and political force. In the course of illustrating its power over most of the vital aspects of society and economy, I will attempt to describe and analyze those characteristics of public bureaucracy which have brought it to the eminence which I claim for it. First, however, I will make an attempt to describe how *homo bureaucratus* interacts with public organizations.

Modes of Interaction

Citizen

The most generalized and venerable notion of interaction between a person and his government is the concept of citizenship. The idea of

[2] See Robert A. Dahl, *Who Governs?* (New Haven: Yale University Press, 1961), pp. 224–227, for a characterization of political man and his apolitical counterpart *Homo Civicus*.

citizenship has enjoyed a powerful position in American political ideology. Citizenship, one learns early on, entails certain rights and privi-
leges, among which are the election of representatives, payment of taxes,
and obedience to the law of the land. Citizenship is a global notion
encompassing a kind of continuing interaction between rulers and ruled
which assumes knowledgeability and interest in things governmental on
the part of the ruled and a healthy respect for the rule of law and election
returns on the part of the rulers. The scope of citizen interest is supposed
to be broad, and those who legislate on its behalf are to be aware of the
conflict between the representation of the public interest and the representation of special interests. Mechanisms devised by the Founding
Fathers and later architects of constitutionalism were meant to deal with
such conflicts. In case mechanisms for the insurance of the representation
of the public interest faltered, the doctrine of judicial review was created
to make certain that the public interest under the rule of law as provided
by the Constitution was in fact adhered to. These structural devices and
others were created to insure an interactive process which was so lacking
in eighteenth-century European monarchies.

Today, citizenship as an interactive means for insuring that the will
of the people is translated into policies and laws has lost much of its
meaning. The contemporary status of citizenship seems most significant
in symbolic terms. People vote, pay taxes, and comply with rules and
laws for a variety of reasons, many of which are justified by belief in
the conception of citizenship as outlined above. The symbolic aspects
of citizenship provide psychological gratification by giving people feelings of efficacy, patriotism, and the general illusion of participation.

But as an active element in the formation of public policy, the concept leaves much to be desired. Except in the smallest electoral units, the
sequence that begins with a vote for a candidate and ends with a policy
change is seldom discoverable. The voice of the citizenry can rarely be
directly heard on any given issue. Occasionally, policy outcomes are influenced by politicians and bureaucrats who fear the possible reaction of
the entire citizenry. But as a whole, the attention and concern of the
citizenry are either highly segmented or too diffuse to translate into
policies.

One finds that the modern idea of citizenship is associated more with
loyalty to country and willingness to comply with laws and rules than
with participation. If citizenship is too diffuse a notion to explain the way
people interact with their government, how then might one conceive of
the idea? A central contention of this book is that citizenship is most

significantly ~~experienced by people~~ as bureaucratic constituents, clients, and victims. I identify these as interaction modes; "mode" is taken to mean both the form of interaction and the frequency of its occurrence.

Constituent

The representation of a geographically defined group of people is the usual sense in which the term "constituency" is used. One recalls the Burkean legislator's problem of choosing between that which will benefit all and that which will benefit only the legislator's constituency. Hanna Pitkin summarizes the range of positions on this matter:[3]

A number of positions have at one time or another been defended between the two poles of mandate and independence. A highly restrictive mandate theorist might maintain that true representation occurs only when the representative acts on explicit instructions from his constituents, that any exercise of discretion is a deviation from this ideal. A more moderate position might be that the representative may exercise some discretion, but must consult his constituents before doing anything new or controversial, and then do as they wish or resign. A still less extreme position might be that the representative may act as he thinks his constituents would want, unless or until he receives instructions from them, and then he must obey. Very close to the independence position would be the argument that the representative must do as he thinks best, except insofar as he is bound by campaign promises or an election platform. At the other end is the idea of complete independence, that constituents have no right even to extract campaign promises; once a man is elected he must be completely free to use his own judgment.

If one applies Pitkin's description to groups constituted in a number of ways and arraying themselves among a variety of pertinent issue constellations, then how and to whom are interests likely to be represented? The politics of *intra*organizational representation are likely to be guided by a set of norms very different from those characteristic of elected constituency representatives.

Such voluntary associations as clubs, veterans groups, some professional societies, "public" interest groups, conservationists, manufacturers' organizations, and some unions represent the interests of their member-

---

[3] Hanna Pitkin, *The Concept of Representation* (Berkeley: University of California Press, 1967), p. 146.

ship according to a variety of loose and tangentially "democratic" procedures. Often the mechanisms of such organizationally "democratic" voluntary organizations include polls of opinion and election of officers. The trappings of democracy, however, are often its fullest realization; the common situation is domination by elites of the internal workings of the organization as well as of its representation to the external environment.[4] Such elites often consist of the most interested members of the organization. Their interest is fueled by (among other things) needs to enhance their personal social status, wealth, or potential for influence inside and outside the organizational framework. Representation of interests, which tend toward maximal inclusivity according to elite perception, occurs when the threat of elite displacement is substantial or when there is a significant value consensus between leaders and followers.

The benefits of labor union membership and membership in other economic associations that represent their members' interests do not necessarily include every member; and of those who are beneficiaries, not all share equally as a result of membership. Mancur Olson has dealt with the question of collective and noncollective goods and service provision in the context of economic groups like labor unions and trade associations.[5] At this point it seems sufficient to say that membership in an organization which actively seeks to promote organizational interests as well as those of its individual members does not necessarily maximize individual benefits.

Group membership of a voluntary (and quasi-voluntary) nature is a central concern for many scholars who deal with the nature of representation in American politics.[6] Lobbying, pressure through advertising,

---

[4] The literature on the oligarchic nature of private government leadership is extensive and goes back well into the last century in the writing of Michels, for instance. The general question is addressed in Sanford Lakoff and Daniel Rich, eds., *Private Government* (Glenview, Ill.: Scott, Foresman, 1973). For a famous exception to the general proposition proffered here, see Lipset, Trow, and Coleman's *Union Democracy* (Glencoe, Ill.: Free Press, 1956). Lipset takes a more general look at the question of the political process in unions and arrives at conclusions which are not significantly different from the ones presented here in his *Political Man* (New York: Doubleday, 1960), Chapter 12.

[5] Mancur Olson, *The Logic of Collective Action* (Cambridge, Mass.: Harvard University Press, 1971).

[6] Robert A. Dahl, *A Preface to Democratic Theory* (Chicago: University of Chicago Press, 1956); Theodore J. Lowi, *The End of Liberalism* (New York: W. W. Norton, 1969); E. E. Schattschneider, *The Semi-Sovereign People* (New York: Holt, 1960); Arthur F. Bentley, *The Process of Government* (Bloomington: Principia,

campaign contributions, letter writing campaigns, and a variety of other techniques characterize the actions of such voluntary and quasi-voluntary groups. This distinction is arbitrarily drawn to distinguish between, say, the NAACP and a teamster local; membership in the NAACP is usually a matter of preference, but membership in the teamster local is a condition of employment.

As government became involved in new and different aspects of economic and social life during the twentieth century, the locus and character of constituency representation changed. While legislative constituencies remained significant, a new kind of relationship began to evolve at the administrative level. Indeed, the continued well-being and growth of some cabinet level agencies became linked more to servicing their constituents than to anything else.

The most obvious example of this phenomenon is the Department of Agriculture. Its organizational history and development in many ways epitomize the creation of that most significant evolving constituency–government relationship: the bureaucratic one. Grant McConnell[7] has written most eloquently on the subject. He argues that farmers had little expectation of exercising much "voice" (to borrow Albert Hirschman's term)[8] in either political party at the end of the last century. That is not to say that the farm vote was not a potent factor in the calculations of politicians at the national level, but rather that the farm voice was one of many, often conflicting, voices. A narrowing of the focus of voice in national policy and a change in the institutional setting for its exercise occurred which had serious consequences for the representation of agricultural interests.

The Department of Agriculture reached into the vast geography of the nation in the form of thousands of county agents. The most powerful agricultural interest group was the Farm Bureau which was not a "general farm group," but rather a highly skilled lobby which had organized a "farm bloc" in Congress. McConnell's description of bureaucratic constituency organization and representation through county agents provides one with an almost classic map of the reformulated idea of constituency.[9]

1949); David Truman, *The Governmental Process* (New York: Knopf, 1951); and Pitkin, *The Concept of Representation*.

[7] Grant McConnell, *Private Power and American Democracy* (New York: Knopf, 1967).

[8] Albert O. Hirschman, *Exit, Voice and Loyalty* (Cambridge, Mass.: Harvard University Press, 1970).

[9] McConnell, *Private Power and American Democracy*, pp. 232–233.

. . . Most agents were publicly paid organizers and functionaries of the Farm Bureaus; at the same time they were the Department of Agriculture's only field service across the nation. In theory public and private servants concurrently, the county agents were effectively immune from Department orders and domination. The substantial national support given to the extension system was funneled through grants-in-aid to the states. Only trivial federal restrictions went with these gifts. The agencies for state supervision of the agents were the land-grant colleges of agriculture, which maintained their own independence from political direction. Even within the colleges, the extension system tended to be rather autonomous. In effect, then, the agents were most closely tied to the local counties in which they worked, where they were beholden to county government and even more to the Farm Bureaus they had organized and which they served as partial employees. Officially, their status was more ambiguous: they were national, state, and local officials; they were also privately employed. Informally, however, there was little doubt where their effective political responsibility lay—to the locally influential farmers. And these were well-knit into the Farm Bureaus.

Several important themes of bureaucratic constituency are tied together here. Clearly, the representation of the interests of the Farm Bureaus is paramount both for the Department of Agriculture and for the farm bloc in Congress. The role of representative is that of a nonelected public official known as a county agent and who is beholden to private interests in a relationship sanctioned by law. McConnell clearly contends, furthermore, that local Farm Bureaus were dominated by the most powerful farmers.

The confusion of jurisdictional authorities, which is a property of federalism, and the "nonpolitical" character of colleges were perfect ground for the development of a system that thoroughly obliterates the public–private distinction and that permits the domination of national policy by those who are most likely to be affected by it. Not only can one readily observe the possibilities of conflict of interest being elevated to a status of institutional legitimacy, but one can also perceive the idea of constituency being reduced to a system of representation of the powerful in the name of the many.

McConnell's description exemplifies the point that the meaning of bureaucratic constituency tends to have an aspect of classical corporatism. In other words, the organizational form which is the primary constituent of the agency has the common characteristic of private formal organization in which members receive the benefits of membership without being able to specify or alter significantly the nature of those benefits. Indeed, the assumption is that what is good for the powerful farmer is good for all farmers. Furthermore, one can infer that what is good for Farm Bureau elites is good for the Department of Agriculture and for the general public. The constituency of the Department of Agriculture is issue-specific; that is, it tends to concern itself with matters salient to agricultural policy and those policies which affect agriculture, and it tends to be a self-governing entity operating with the full blessings of law and custom.

What of the nonpowerful member of the Farm Bureau and the farmer who doesn't even belong to the organization? McConnell draws some strong conclusions about this in his general statement about private power. He argues that the cost of such private aggregations of public power is great in terms of the ideal of representation of constituency interests.[10]

The recognition of a right of autonomy, self-determination, or self-regulation may be expedient, given the group's power. But it does not eliminate the power over its members which the leadership of the group may have; indeed, it is more likely than not to enhance that power. When, under the guise of serving an ideal of democracy as the self-government of small units, the coercive power of public authority is given to these groups, their internal government becomes a matter of serious concern.

What we know of the internal government of such groups substantiates McConnell's argument for the most part. Hierarchies that provide little or no opportunity for effective bottom-up representation or accountability seem to characterize most large private organizations linked in a constituency relationship to public agencies.

As a general proposition, then, a bureaucratic constituent is usually a formal organization that is interdependent with a public bureaucracy. Interdependence in this sense means the surrender of power for mutual benefit.[11] Thus, the ability of the public bureaucracy to act depends in large measure upon the agreement of its constituencies. Constituents of

10 Ibid., pp. 341–342.

11 James D. Thompson in *Organizations in Action* (New York: McGraw-Hill, 1967) reformulates the notion of interdependence suggested by Richard M. Emerson, "Power-Dependence Relations," *American Sociological Review* (February, 1962), 31–40.

public agencies are similarly constrained in their actions. Bureaucratic constituents in general are policy-specific and possess resources that give them the potential to threaten incumbent bureaucrats.

Agriculture constituents, for example, concern themselves with issues and policies that directly affect them; they are unlikely to dissipate their attention and energies in nonagricultural areas. The resources they have which may be used to threaten the Agriculture Department include influence over certain congressmen, senators, and governors through campaign contributions, propaganda, and bloc voting. The USDA has an arsenal of its own (e.g., administrative rule making, professionalized expertise, budgetary initiative).

In an important sense, institutions within the formal boundaries of the state can themselves be understood to be bureaucratic constituents. When congressmen and senators find themselves dependent upon bureaucracies for perfectly legal discretionary administrative actions, they become in effect bureaucratic constituents. For instance, those who trade votes with bureaucrats in exchange for favorable treatment in their districts in order to enhance their reelection chances are interdependent with public bureaucracies. In the realms of political economy and national defense, I will illustrate how bureaucracies can build constituency relationships inside as well as outside the formal boundaries of government.

Client

The term "client" as used here refers to a person or group of people who are dependent upon a patron, in this case a governmental patron. A client differs from a constituent individual or group primarily because the client is not significantly able to alter the behavior of his (or its) bureaucratic patron, but the constituent individual or group may indeed be able to influence outcomes of the policy process. Collectively organized constituents (like labor unions) may be called a *descriptive group insofar as group actions in the political arena in some ways characterize the manifest wishes of some or all members of the constituency. The ascriptive character of clientele groups (like the poor) arises out of their identification by bureaucrats and politicians in terms of a set of attributes which individuals possess but which do not constitute a basis upon which they organize themselves for collective action.* Indeed, clients tend not to organize for the representation of interests. A clientele is an aggregation of individuals and groups that interacts in a dependent fashion with one or more government agencies. Clients do not normally represent even a potential threat to public bureaucracy, but constituent groups do.

The needs and wants of a clientele are likely to be effectively made by public officials rather than by privately organized claimants. The needs and wants of clientele are most often articulated in the professionalized social welfare and control structures of public organizations. Although this may also be true of a constituency, the bureaucratic advocate's articulation of interest is unlikely to be a response to demand external to the public agency. Intra-agency professionals decide what client "demand" is according to some combination of professional and agency standards.

My reformulation of constituency involves an incomplete transfer of a traditional legislative–electoral concept to a new institutional focus. In some ways the idea of clientele in the bureaucratic context resembles the doctor–patient relationship. A patient is dependent upon the rituals and practices of the medical profession which render him almost powerless before the physician. One may find another doctor, even a quack, but one cannot usually find an organization that competes with government. If doctors had constituents, they would have to give serious attention to the possibility of their being removed or their decisions being overridden by others. Patients can (sometimes) go elsewhere if they are displeased with the physician. Bureaucratic clients have no such market possibilities except under conditions of interbureaucratic competition. In that situation, the clientele of the loser may be attached to the winner without any expectation that the clientele as here defined would raise objection.

Although I have stipulated that one can think of clients both as groups and as individuals, it is the latter form in which one can most easily discover clientele relationships. Welfare recipients tend to be the clients of social workers in the employ of some large public organization or another. AFDC mothers may have demands, requests, needs, and wants, but they are defined (and thus either recognized or ignored) by public employees who act under a set of rules not created or even influenced by the recipient. Indeed, the public employee who actually administers the rules may have had as little to do with their creation as the client. Farm organizations sit down with legislators and administrators and carefully assist them in the formulation of rules governing a variety of interactions which may affect the lives of the farmers represented. Not all farmers and not all farmers' interests are represented, but some are. In regard to public welfare, one may describe many influences on the history of welfare legislation without ever describing the group constituency process or the role of citizenship.[12]

Those groups which tend to be identified as collectivities by virtue of sharing a common ascriptive characteristic, such as being poor, are a crucial part of the "environment" of that vast element of government activity called "social welfare." The poor, the young, and the infirm are the most obvious clientele groups dependent upon government. Since they are either completely unorganized or ineffectively organized, they have no direct influence on policy making.

Perhaps less easily identified are those clients who are neither old, young, poor, nor sick. Postal patrons, auto licensees and registrants, and those who pay taxes are also clients, but episodically so. At one time or another during our lives each of us becomes a client. The agencies connected with these relationships are under most conditions correctly perceived as "purposive machines"[13] which process the paper necessary to continue our lives. Failure to conform to the rules of such processors or a mistake on the part of the agency itself brings penalties upon the client. Like taxation, one's ability to obtain redress or correction varies according to one's resources. If one has little time and money, one makes a more costly expenditure of those resources than a wealthy person does to retrieve an important letter, straighten out a problem with the IRS, or transfer title to an automobile. If one has one's secretary or lawyer "handle" these matters, one is not likely to notice the costs. If, however,

[12] The work of Frances Fox Piven and Richard A. Cloward is very interesting to me as an illumination of the constituency-client distinction drawn here. In their *Regulating the Poor* (New York: Random House, 1971), they trace public welfare history in functional and economic terms. I read them to affirm what I describe as a cliental relationship and find poignant confirmation of this view in their "crisis" solution to the "welfare mess." Briefly, they suggest that organizing all the eligible poor for purposes of flooding the welfare agencies with clients would bring the system to a halt and compel an alteration in present policies. They argue (see p. 321 of *Regulating the Poor*) that this strategy would result in a minimum income program financed nationally. The strategy is essentially an attempt at mobilizing clients rather than attempting to convert clients to constituents. They (correctly, I think) saw the rules of the bureaucracy as the only lever or means for representation of interests of the poor.

[13] J. D. Thompson, *Organizations in Action*, pp. 16–17, identifies such organizations as having "mediating" core technologies. He says ". . . mediating technology requires operating in standardized ways and extensively; e.g., with multiple clients or customers distributed in time and space."

one is unfortunate enough to become a permanent or semipermanent member of a public agency clientele network, then the matter of costs and potential costs is more serious.

Few clients have sufficient resources to consider attempting to transform a clientele into a constituency. The public agency often has the resources necessary for life itself or its continued maintenance at a "reasonable" level. Clients are resources of the agency which serves them, as are constituents, but they are passive resources which public agencies normally cannot or will not mobilize even for the greater power and glory of the organization.

A clientele is represented in the policy process by the agency responsible for it. The professionalization of social service personnel, educators, and medical people explains much about the idea of clientele. These professions are involved in discretionary classification routines which permit only a limited amount and scope of interaction between the client and the patron bureaucracy. Instead of citizens or constituents, people are defined and responded to in terms of the initial category typification most readily dealt with by the professional. "Student," "patient," "AFDC mother," "indigent," and "vagrant" are labels that are useful in defining and acting upon individuals who have (or are) problems.

These individuals surrender to discretionary classification when they define themselves or are defined by others as being in need of help. Discretionary classification routines are those rules followed by individual practitioners of any profession to determine, diagnose, or judge an aspect of another whose "problem" is perceived by the practitioner as coming within the purview of his profession and the administrative rules which constrain it. Once such routines are fixed in the mind and eye of the beholder through education, training, and peer reinforcement, the possibility of the beholden's altering them is difficult to imagine outside of fiction. Clients thus defined by one who is backed by the power of profession and the legitimacy of the state are likely to act and be acted upon in a manner consistent with the "doctor knows best" stereotype.

These routines begin processes that set formal and informal limits on interactions which are appropriate to the client's needs and to the expectations of the professional. One interesting aspect of the client–professional relationship is that it is conceived by both actors as being outside the political process. In other words, the large group of citizens who meet at the vague boundaries of public organizations as professionals and as clients manage a definitional exercise that appears to remove their behaviors from politics.

There is much in popular political belief that protects us from describing client–professional relationships as being political. Without going into the variety of ways one can conceive of the political, one can suggest that public agencies involved in allocative decisions within the framework of agency-generated rules are engaged in a political process. The public character seems to not matter in client-centered situations as described above. Yet one might be remiss in failing to identify as political those aspects of rule making, enforcement, and adjudication which directly affect both the client who receives the service and the aggregate which provides the resources. It should be stressed that the ancient administration/politics dichotomy is not being suggested, but rather a newer phenomenon. Clients have their lives influenced in important ways by professionals who act with the authority of expertise and the legitimacy of the state. The same situation does not pertain to constituency relationships. The AFL–CIO hires economists from the same outstanding graduate institutions that the Treasury and Department of Labor customarily patronize. Such "balancing of experts" is not part of the client–professional relationship.

The debate over public/private and policy/administration distinctions perhaps becomes more useful at the level of the descriptive client organization. Client organizations are here defined as those collective entities whose existence is predicated wholly or in great part on the patronage of a government agency. For example, one might point to the hundreds of firms that engage in no other activity but supplying the Department of Defense with some specialized good or service. The number of specialized firms that are agency dominated because of spatial or locational factors is difficult to estimate. But one need only visit a large government installation in an isolated area to see the web of motel owners, food franchisers, and so on, totally dependent upon trade created by the agency. They have little if any voice in the conduct of agency affairs appropriate to them. Indeed, like the saloon owner who fears being declared off-limits to military personnel, such spatially relevant private firms may be understood as extensions or satellites of the agency which enforce agency norms and conform to whatever extraterritorial rules the agency lays down.

Functionally defined client organizations exist in nonmarket situations to the extent that they have little or no private sector interactions. Manufacturers of hardware for defense, space exploration, and avionic purposes are ready examples of client organizations. Usually, these are small-scale manufacturers who are separated from the patron agency, in part because of ideological rigidities that normally forbid government agencies from manufacturing goods. The distinction between a patron agency and its client organization is meaningful in terms of costs and legalities, not in terms of organizational power or policy. Such client organizations are creatures of the patron. When the patron is healthy, they flourish; when the patron suffers reverses (as NASA did in the late 1960s and early 1970s), they either die or they develop other kinds of businesses.

Client organizations and people who are clients are at least beneficiaries of organizational outputs. In the case of an economic client organization, accumulated benefits over time could put the firm in a position to diversify sufficiently to reduce or negate the potential effects of the withdrawal of agency patronage. Even individual cliental relationships create the possibility of alternate sources of support, although such possibilities may be dim indeed. The modal client of public agencies probably can expect a dependency of substantial duration. One can conceive of clientele networks, which consist of unorganized individuals, mobilizing into some sort of constituency-like group. Patients in veterans' hospitals could conceivably enlist the support of the American Legion and VFW in order to improve services and conditions in VA hospitals. Such things are imaginable, but they are not likely to endure beyond the resolution of the issue (or issues). The final interaction mode admits of no such potentiality for representation of interest.

Victim

Millions of Americans live a daily struggle to obtain the necessities for minimal existence. Hunger and the other deprivations of poverty define one class of victims. The very bottom of the egg-shaped structure of American society exerts absolutely no direct influence over the actions of public organizations. The policies of such organizations not only define the conditions of existence and the possible modes of interaction for this population, but they also decide vital personal matters without ever having interacted with those affected. These people have their lives altered as a function of the "aggregate" effect of policy or policies. They are the "unanticipated consequences" of urban renewal policies, food stamp administration, drug control programs, and regulatory acts in general.

Victims are not clients. They are a nameless mass whose destiny is subject to forces created by policy implementation. Victims, unlike those of us whose lives are episodically bounded by policy outcomes and public agency regulation, live existences highly dependent upon public policy decisions which take place beyond their consciousnesses. Those in our midst who cannot obtain minimal education, employment, food, or shelter are essentially bereft of resources, and their inability to obtain these resources is to some greater or lesser extent a result of governmental activity.

Whether government has a responsibility to provide the minima of existence is not a question germane to this particular argument. Victims, as I am defining them, are relevant to policy outcomes simply because of the pervasiveness of the governmental presence in post-industrial society. Insofar as government creates positive or negative externalities which have impact on the minima of existence, it creates victims as mindlessly as it may create beneficiaries. (Externalities are the unintended economic and social effects of government action.) Victimization is more than a simple extension of the idea of the relatively powerless client. One might reasonably argue that the extension of negative externalities to clients may end in victimization. The argument presented here is that part of the population identified as victims of aggregate policy outcomes are totally passive actors whose identity is more readily described statistically than in interactive terms. Indeed, it may even be inappropriate to discuss these victims *interactively* at all.

Victims of aggregate policy outcomes are acted upon by changes in the economic and social environment which occur as a partial result of government activity. The existence of the group itself is an ascriptive exercise, since one cannot easily locate such a residual category of humanity in the literature of public policy. By residual category, I mean to suggest that aggregate policy victims are most easily defined as those who receive little or no food on a daily basis, whose children receive little or no education, who live in conditions of minimal shelter and sanitation, and who do not interact with government, except as objects.

Those who are the objects of government policy seldom know that they are the objects of government policy. The "poor," as conceived of by politicians and bureaucrats of the 1960s, were usually anonymous. Indeed, the "discovery" of the poor by the War on Poverty Programs was in many ways an exercise in defining an ascriptive class, followed by an attempt to mobilize members of that class into clients, and perhaps even constituents.[14] While the program may have failed, at the very least it did highlight one segment of the forgotten millions directly affected by policy outcomes who are here identified as victims. To be sure, not all the poor are victims. Many are clients and some are constituents. Those who are neither are simply passive recipients of environmental changes which are in part determined by the actions of public agencies.

There are victims of public agency outputs who are all too aware of the rules, regulations, and demands of government. Those who are defined as insane, mentally retarded, or alcoholic are not likely to enjoy even a cliental relationship, if they are inmates of public institutions. Mental institutions, public hospitals, juvenile prisons, and other caretaker agencies are often not much different from maximum security institutions or cemeteries for the living. One simple way to dispose of such persons intellectually is to define them as something less than human and therefore not the proper subject for a discussion of the ways in which members of society interact with the most visible parts of the government they supposedly control. What a distance from citizen to mental patient! If one simply argues that citizenship is minimally defined in terms of individual rights of freedom to speak, move about, own property and the like, subject to the codes of civil and criminal law, then the status of mental patients who have violated no law and who are not incarcerated voluntarily becomes rather a nice intellectual question.[15]

The presence of total institutions in a democratic society has long been an analytical anomaly.[16] The removal of some members of society from the possibility of exercising minimal rights of citizenship is normally justified and understood in terms of the urgent need being met by the organization of which the citizen is a member (i.e., crew member of a ship in wartime) or because of the potential danger to society, should members of the institution be allowed public freedom (i.e., mental patients, convicted felons). Perhaps there is something worth the note of

[14] For a more complete argument on the subject, see Eugene Lewis, *The Urban Political System* (Hinsdale, Ill.: Dryden, 1973), pp. 256–266.

[15] Thomas S. Szasz, *The Myth of Mental Illness* (New York: Delta, 1961).

[16] David J. Rothman, *The Discovery of the Asylum* (Boston: Little, Brown, 1971). This is a very important historical work that deals with a variety of total institutions created in the zeal of early nineteenth-century reform. He discusses the creation and development of almshouses, workhouses, lunatic asylums, and penitentiaries. In this day of "psychiatric justice" and crimes without victims, such historical analysis is very helpful to the political scientist who would try to place nondemocratic public institutions in contemporary settings.

political scientists in understanding the popularity of two novels of the 1960s which describe two public agencies attempting to exercise total control over their nonvoluntary membership. Many students have perceived the protagonists of *Catch-22* and *One Flew Over the Cuckoo's Nest* as being metaphorical equivalents of post-industrial man confronting society itself as if it were a total institution. Certainly part of that construction of reality can be understood to describe the category which we have identified as victims.

Victimization in the second sense (i.e., the direct action of public agencies upon persons as objects) is normally a function of the police power (i.e., health, safety, and welfare) of government. In America, orphans, the physically and mentally handicapped, the poor, some of the aged, the criminal, and the indigent have historically been the responsibility of the states and municipalities. The federal government has entered the field only lately. At the local level the most common discoverer and creator of victims (of crimes and of government) are the police. Policemen deal with the widest range of human behavior normally confronted by any representative of public bureaucracy. The discretionary classification routines they follow and their ability to enforce them differentially have been the subject of much study in the past ten years.[17] It is not news that the poor, the black, the young, the indigent, and the ignorant are treated differently by the police. They are also victims, as we have defined them, because for all practical purposes, when they are arrested or have their homes or persons searched, they have little practical recourse for redress of grievance.

Police occupy a unique position as agents of public authority in regard to the question of individual interaction with government. The criminal justice system in general tends to create organizational victims by virtue of the differential enforcement of the law, the bail system, and the arrest of social deviants and "criminals without victims." Drug users, prostitutes, alcoholics, homosexuals, and other social deviants become victims, not only by the laws that make them criminal, but also by the differential possibilities of arrest. White, wealthy, and middle-aged homosexuals, alcoholics, or drug users seldom suffer the stigma of arrest and conviction. The capacity to arrest and stigmatize is basic to the

---

[17] James Q. Wilson, *Varieties of Police Behavior* (Cambridge: Harvard University Press, 1968) and Jerome H. Skolnick, *Justice Without Trial* (New York: Wiley, 1966). These two studies, among hundreds of others, make the point in different ways, I believe.

coercive power of the state to create victims. Such victim creation is almost always an act of administrative discretion by a public agent, the policeman. Thus, within the ancient and honorable obligation of the state to maintain public order and to arrest criminals fall those discretionary possibilities for creating the role of victim, as I have restrictively used the term.

Two kinds of victims have been generally identified: (1) those who are indirectly victimized by macroscopic negative externalities (like inflation) generated by the action of public agencies and (2) those who are directly confronted by a public agency that exercises the power to effectively deny them their basic constitutional rights. Representation of these victims is held to be strictly an internal bureaucratic matter, the concern of the press, or political officials. In no circumstance short of open rebellion is it to be expected that victims ever represent their own wishes, wants, or needs.

Recapitulation and Synthesis

What might one reasonably infer to be the dimensions underlying these distinctions (citizen, constituent, client, victim)? Efficacy and the sense of efficacy have been matters of direct or implied concern in discussion of each interaction mode. *Efficacy is the power to produce intended results. The sense of efficacy implies a belief about one's ability to so produce.* It has been argued thus far that efficacy is improbable on the part of citizens, is probable for the elites who govern most constituencies, is highly unlikely for clients, and is absent for victims.

I have discussed the *sense of efficacy* in terms of representation. Representation takes place in public bureaucracy in a way most appropriate to the narrowly defined descriptive interests or ascriptive characteristics of constituents, clients, and victims. The notion of the citizenry aggregated for representational purposes seems a wistful artifact of a probably nonexistent past. Constituent organizations tend to have control over those who represent them within public organizations. *Members* of constituent organizations, however, tend to have their interests represented by generally unresponsive, dominant intraorganizational elites. Clients have their interests represented for them, but their interests are authoritatively reinterpreted by the mediating symbols of the professionalized agencies that dominate them. Occasionally, clients can look like constituents or be made to look like constituents, but the normal case is official reinterpretation of client interest. The interests of victims are defined totally by those given the mandate for their control.

Finally, an effort has been made to assess the dependency of each of the classes of interaction upon the agency or agencies to which it is most appropriate. Citizenship continues to be a notion so diffuse as to make it meaningless to this analysis. Except in the aggregate, where all agencies are interdependent with the entire citizenry, and in rare cases of citizen attentiveness to a single issue, the idea of citizen as a mode of interaction has little meaning. The category must not be excluded from the discussion, however; the idea of citizenship is not a straw man of intellectual pretension; it is a powerful symbolic typification, common to the culture and to the literature of politics and public administration. There are those who believe that the citizenry's sense of political efficacy underpins the political order to a substantial degree. Further, while citizenship appears not terribly useful as an interaction mode, the concept of citizenship may be a significant and general received value of those who dominate the policy process.

Constituents are interdependent with their ruling organizational or institutional elites. The definition of the term "constituent" at the macroscopic level implies mutuality of benefit, although the relationship between agency and constituency may not always be equal in benefit and power. Normally, the client is a supplicant whose needs and/or wants can be satisfied only by agency action. The client's dependency is mitigated at a general level by the absolute need of professionalized agencies to have clientele in order to justify their existences. Usually, however, the client, unlike the constituent, has few resources with which to create a truly interdependent relationship with the agency. The client is likely to have ascribed characteristics (like being poor) appropriate to the discretionary classification (he qualifies for aid or he does not) routines of the professionalized bureaucrats who interact with him.

Victims occupy two logically obvious categories: they are either intentional victims or they are unintentional victims. For instance, at the moment this is being written, the bottom one-fifth of the socioeconomic structure of America (an ascriptive group) seems to be suffering the unintended, unfortunate consequences of macroeconomic policy decisions made several years ago by various high-level federal officials. The social world that this bottom one-fifth confronts is bounded and shaped by government action over time. As government agencies identify more conditions in the social order in need of governmental intervention, it becomes easier to substantiate the claim that large numbers of people who do not directly interact with any agency on a long-term basis are nevertheless profoundly affected by the complex environmental impact of agency policies. This is particularly so of that group of interactions characteristic of victims.

One might read these pages and conclude that he has at one time or another experienced some or all of the interactive modes. This is not an unreasonable conclusion. It suggests that our relationship with government is dependent upon a set of contingencies set in time and space rather than upon some transcendent and enduring form of interaction. This is so for many of us. For millions of others, however, the distinctions drawn here do indeed constitute modal points of enduring interaction with the political system. Indeed, for many these typifications may be the labels most appropriate for understanding the relationships between the rulers and the ruled.

Thus an hypothesis: Citizenship is most accurately described by the behaviors of public bureaucracies and the constituent, client, and victim networks with which they interact. This hypothesis may be elaborated by a more careful summary of some key dimensions that separate the modes of interaction. These are sketched below and are summarized in Table 1–1.

Table 1–1   Citizenry–Bureaucracy Relationships

Dimensions of Interaction	Interaction Modes		
	Constituent	Client	Victim
Character of interest representation	Highly focused; locationally, functionally specific	Highly focused; authoritatively reinterpreted	Disembodied
Efficacy: power to alter policy outcomes	Great	Little	None
Efficacy: upon a public agency for viability	Interdependence	Nearly complete	Total

1. *The character of interest representation.* The assumption is that the interests of persons appropriate to a particular public agency are represented and that the specificity and location of that representation are politically significant and empirically discoverable.
2. *Efficacy: the power to alter outcomes.* The question here is does the population described have the (legal, political, or economic) power to (a) initiate or prevent the appearance of a serious item on the agency agenda and/or (b) initiate or prevent successful implementation once a policy decision has been reached?
3. *Dependence upon a public agency for viability.* If dependency connotes the obverse of power and interdependence connotes the surrender of power for mutual benefit, then a reasonable question about the modes of interaction entails a consideration of whether the bureaucratic dog wags the public tail or *vice versa.* Our analysis suggests that the question seems as inappropriate for the "citizen" category as it seems self-evident for the "victim" category. The difficulty is not so much with the dimension as it is with the general theoretical premises available to deal with the relationships between the polity and public organizations. In any case, the viability dimension attempts to answer the empirical question: can those most closely identified with the mode of interaction survive (literally and figuratively) if the public agency upon which they depend either ceases to exist or radically alters its relevant outputs?

Major questions arise out of the claims made thus far. If it is true that America is a nation of bureaucratic constituents, clients, and victims, then what sort of general conceptual framework might help one account for this situation? If the conceptual framework is descriptive, then how does it operate and how has it come into existence?

Chapter two attempts to deal with the first question and the ensuing chapters with the latter questions.

chapter two

A Conceptual Framework:
Realms, Mixes,
Politics, and Policies

The Realm of the Political

An understanding of how we came to live in a world dominated by public bureaucracy necessarily involves a consideration of what we mean when we identify things as political. When forced to provide a single sentence definition, I identify politics as *conflict and cooperation by powerful actors over the allocation of scarce public resources.* This formulation is rooted in the belief that definitional exercises about politics ought to revolve around certain key concepts which focus our attention on questions of *public* resources. Power, scarce resources, and the processes of conflict and cooperation are not concepts which necessarily limit one's understanding of the political to include only the actions of the state. Because of the variety of meanings attached to the terms used in this book, an exercise in definition is called for. One stipulates (attaches a special meaning to a term) in order to proceed with analysis. A realm of the political (*that place in time and space where politics takes place*) and the concept of politics itself cannot easily be put to rest by the dictionary or by dictionary-like definition.

Stipulation is difficult precisely because institutional and individual actors both in and out of the political realms are engaged in a constant struggle to control the definition of politics. The conundrum is that the definition of politics and the location of the realms of the political are some of the basic issues of politics as well as of political philosophy. The form of the conflict and its location is highly varied. There are those who believe that politics is to be discovered in families, firms, boy scout troops, and almost any place where human interaction occurs. Most people seem to be comfortable with terms like "office politics." "Campus politics," "playing politics" or "being very political" conjure images of cunning, calculation, and private motives hiding behind contrary public postures. We must dispense with these meanings and pursue a stipulation of politics and its realms which permits us to understand something about the evolving relationship between the individual and the state if our analysis is to proceed.

The test of the definitional exercise is not its truth or beauty in isolation, but whether or not it is useful in understanding how actors behave politically and in what context that behavior is to be discovered. I begin with the idea of the state as an entity with physical presence in the form of persons and resources. The key resource of the state is its ability to command compliance through the actions of those who represent it. The state is the single entity which can through law and by persuasion, acquiescence, or coercion compel *all* persons to obey it. The resources of the state are enormous and include money, organization, and legitimacy-creating symbols which are brought to bear in order to control individual and institutional behavior. (Legitimacy-creating symbols include laws, the flag, democratic procedures and any visual or other representation of the state to which people have some degree of emotional commitment.)

Individual persons and collectivities engaging in patterns of conflict and cooperation over the control of some or all aspects of the state and its resources are engaged in politics. Where they engage in this activity and how they engage in it are themselves matters of political controversy. The results of conflict and cooperation over the allocation of some scarce public resource (including definitions of the political) I shall call policies. Politics and the policies which emerge from it have over the history of the Republic tended to drift in directions very different from those envisaged by the Founding Fathers. As indicated in chapter one, it is an hypothesis of this book that the realm of the political is increasingly being defined by actors structured into large-scale, complex public and private organizations. If this hypothesis is to be supported, then we must attempt to discover how, when, where, and why the change is taking place. But first we must explain our meaning of policy and the act of defining the realm of the political as well as politics.

Received Value Mixes: A Concept of Policy and of Structure

To value an object or an idea is to give it worth. The set of behaviors an actor uses to obtain a policy is valuative in that it normally precludes other behaviors and is ordinarily deemed appropriate or inappropriate by competitors and allies. Revolution precludes bargaining in most circumstances, for instance, since it usually involves fundamental or major disruptions of the "normal" process of conflict and cooperation. The "normal process" is as valuative as "revolution." The point is that the rules of the game or the usual processes are themselves the outcomes of politics: in short, they are policies. There is the possibility of terminological difficulty when one attempts to talk about policies which have to do with process and those having to do with substance. There are also important intellectual reasons for further separating the two.

Policies which have to do with defining the proper realm of the political, which have endured over time, and which normally are not active, current matters of conflict are the basis of political structure. Policies which create political structure seldom emerge from competition and conflict as a comprehensive package. If political structure is created all at once, then it is unlikely to endure. Thus, the American Constitution, as comprehensive a set of policies defining the realm of the political as has ever endured, is in the words of a Justice of the Supreme Court "what the judges say it is."[1] Political structure in America derives values from the Constitution, manipulates the symbols of the Constitution, and is limited by people's ideas about the Constitution. But the Constitution did not create contemporary political structure. It is, rather, part of what I shall call a received value mix.

People create political structure. They also receive it from the past. The received value mix which *is* political structure exists in persons and institutions. *The received value mix of contemporary persons and institutions consists of the laws, customs, beliefs, and desires which have animated, regulated, and directed agencies of the state and their constituent and clientele networks in the past.* A received value mix is a much slower

---

[1] Merlo J. Pusey, *Charles Evans Hughes* (New York: Macmillan, 1951), p. 204. Pusey quotes the late Chief Justice as saying: "We are under a Constitution, but the Constitution is what the judges say it is."

moving phenomenon than the policies which people attempt to push through it. It limits and directs people because of their knowledge of it in themselves, in others, and in the organizational contexts in which it becomes institutionalized.

Political structure thought of in terms of slowly changing received value mixes allows us not only to escape from notions of structure which imply rigidity and writ. The concept also permits discussion of *mixes* of values received from the past which may differ not only in people's subjective interpretation of them, but may also differ in different realms of the political. Thus, our analysis includes contrasting received value mixes which typify different realms of the political. Received value mixes may be consistent and may "work" in one realm without any important relationship to other realms within the set of realms making up a political system.

Imagine a proposal that would involve giving every policeman and his family government-paid health insurance and certain educational services during active service and into retirement. Imagine further that he and his family can buy highly discounted necessities as well as many of the luxuries at government stores open only to policemen. Imagine housing allowances, special funding for the schools his children attend, and special hardship allowances for being compelled to live in the city where he works. The argument to support such a system might involve pointing out the risky life a policeman faces, the dislocation and insecurity his family must live with, and the indispensable services he performs for society. The case could go on and on, but any reader familiar with the received value mix of the realm in which policemen are found in American political life will know that this is an impossible proposal, beyond the dreams of even the local police union.

The paternalistic socialism of the example presented above is part of the received value mix of the armed forces of the United States and is only a matter of controversy at the margins of its realm. Peacetime officers and their dependents are no more threatened with death or injury than urban policemen. Even in war the vast majority of modern servicemen do not come very near combat situations. The explanation for such "military socialism" cannot be simply attributed to the function of the armed forces.

One cannot easily identify received values which are at once transcendent and equally significant in all realms. Thus, it is difficult, if not almost impossible, to talk about *the* political structure of the United

States. To think in terms of received value mixes takes us away from rigid images of political structure and from monolithic conceptions of values which typify the entire political system. This is not to argue that inquiries into transcendent political values of the American system are a waste of time. On the contrary, they are important and often valuable, but such analysis does not directly aid in furthering the task at hand.

Policy was defined above as that which results from politics, but more must be said if the concept of received value mixes and the matter of political realms are to be integrated with it. If we are to understand that that which we identify as political structure can best be comprehended by the concept of received value mixes and if the realm of the political is itself a matter of controversy for political actors, how then may one conceive of policy?

Policy and Policy Change

Since the received value mix of any given realm limits and defines the politics of that realm, the question of how the received value mix changes arises. Our definition of the received value mix of any realm contends that it is a *congeries* of law, custom, belief, and desires inherited from the distant and near past; the possibility of conflict, then, is clearly implied. This is so because received values may be internally contradictory, as in the case of an agency responsible for regulating *and* promoting a particular industrial activity (e.g., the old Atomic Energy Commission). Depending to some extent upon the realm, conflict and cooperation occur in the context of "rules of the game" which are part of the received value mix. The "rules of the game" in American politics vary from realm to realm and within realms as well.

During the past five years the Department of Health, Education and Welfare has conducted studies of marijuana and its effects. Recently I watched the *Today* show and heard the Secretary of HEW discuss the latest *Marijuana Report to the President*.[2] The interviewer questioned the Secretary very closely on the findings of the scientists and on his views of

[2] There have been five such *Reports,* beginning with *Marihuana: A Signal of Misunderstanding* (Washington, D.C.: Government Printing Office, 1972). This *Report* was considered to be so controversial, because of its striking deviation from past policy, that President Nixon took the extraordinary action of disavowing it.

their findings. The Secretary was careful to point out that the *Report* was the result of a continuing and painstaking scientific effort to determine the possible benefits and dangers of the drug.

The history of government involvement with this drug is long and involved and is well detailed elsewhere.[3] For our purposes, it is a useful example of some of the concepts that we have defined above. The Secretary's insistence on the scientific nature of the inquiry suggests rather clearly that the values associated with scientific investigation are thoroughly embedded in the mix that characterizes HEW and some of its constituency and clientele networks. He also implied that the scientific research was detached, disinterested, and replicable. Perhaps in very limited terms it might even have been "value free" once laboratory and clinical work had begun. How such a study arose, why it arose, and the context in which it occurs are other questions.

The fact that an agency of the state is responsible for recommending policy choices to other political actors who may then decide to have that very agency and others enforce regulations regarding the sale and use of that drug places the act of scientific investigation squarely in the middle of a set of received value mixes which are political. They are political in the extent to which scarce public resources are allocated for the study, to the extent that many members of other organizations concerned with drug enforcement throughout the nation are affected, and to the extent that the population of marijuana users and those around them can or will alter their behaviors. The political structure of drug regulation and enforcement has changed as powerful actors create zones of conflict between received values. Thus, the act of "discovering" marijuana to be a drug that induced criminal behavior was as political as the evolving "discovery" that it is probably no more dangerous than a variety of other substances whose use is reasonably common and which may even have been encouraged by the state.

The impetus for reappraising marijuana was in part the discovery that millions of people had tried the drug and that millions more were habitual users. The shift of federal concern from various enforcement arms of the government to HEW provides us with an example of powerful actors redefining the nature of the problem because of serious shifts in the environment. It is of the greatest import to citizens, clients, constituents, and victims when the state alters the legal meaning of an act by changing it from a crime to an illness or a matter of private choice.

---

[3] John Kaplan, *Marijuana: The New Prohibition* (New York: New World, 1970).

Clearly, such a shift would have great significance to the hundreds of thousands of policemen, judges, jailors, social workers, and others who regularly deal with marijuana users in terms of the rules, regulations, beliefs, and desires of *their* professions. An account of the shifts in marijuana policy illustrates four sources of policy generation and change.

Received Value Mixes Imply Conflict Through Contradiction

Actors perceive received values differently for a variety of reasons which may have to do with self-interest, altruism, ignorance, or (more likely) vagueness in the mix itself. The disagreement over meaning, appropriateness, or utility by powerful actors within a given political realm is likely to create conflicted zones of received value mixes with the potential for generating political action. Thus, policy can emanate from within a realm when the received value mix contains contradictions which are salient to powerful actors. Received value mixes which contain imperatives to simultaneously regulate, promote, and investigate some aspect of human behavior are most likely to be those which generate policy change based on conflict through contradiction.

Marijuana was defined as a dangerous drug about forty years ago. "Reefer madness," which allegedly followed use of the drug, was popularized by police and prosecutors during the 1930s and can conveniently be understood as having become part of the received value mix in the form of law with passage of the Marijuana Tax Act of 1937. The law became a foundation for the expansion of the role of its main bureaucratic proponents and administrators, the Federal Bureau of Narcotics. The Commissioner, Harry J. Anslinger, in the tradition of aggressive bureaucratic politicians, "made" the drug into a menace through a propaganda campaign which had the effect of building and activating a potential constituency network of sizable proportions. Educators, clergymen, and editorial writers as well as state and local legislators and law enforcement officials were provided with a new basis for legitimating their actions *vis-à-vis* their clients and constituents.

Anslinger and the Bureau of Narcotics grew in power and influence in a manner parallel to J. Edgar Hoover and the FBI. The view of the drug that became embedded in the received value mix throughout the political realm concerned with crime, children, and morality in general is best summarized in the words of Anslinger himself.[4]

---

[4] Ibid., p. 9.

How many murders, suicides, robberies, criminal assaults, holdups, burglaries, and deeds of maniacal insanity it [marijuana] causes each year, especially among the young, can only be conjectured.

Few were in a position to argue the point, and the Bureau successfully set a value of the state where none had *specifically* existed before. Over time this view of the drug became part of the received value mix as the policemen and propagandists of the Bureau repeated the endless cycle of scaring appropriations committees into providing larger portions of the budgetary pie.

wow!. Worms of contradiction, however, lay quietly in the apples of Anslinger's pie. They did not emerge for many years, and I shall discuss below why they emerged. For the moment it is important simply to spot some of the contradictions in the received value mix for purposes of illustrating how these contradictions can become a zone of conflict. One contradiction lies in the question implied by Anslinger's horrifying statement. How many crimes *indeed are caused* by marijuana? The contradictory potential of Anslinger's flat empirical statement is rich precisely because someone may come along and (a) prove that no crimes are caused by the drug or (b) prove that many crimes are caused by it. If either (a) or (b) is demonstrated, then two obvious problems arise through contradiction. If (a) is true, then why allocate resources for the suppression of the drug? If (b) is true, then a relatively puny enforcement agency might have to yield its function either to agencies with massive enforcement and detection capabilities or to agencies which deal with epidemics. The latter is so because Anslinger's identification of the drug as a root cause of crime could easily allow the problem to be conceived of as a medical or public health matter. Speculation about the ramifications of contradictions that become the basis for conflict within this realm could continue. The point is that policy change itself may be discoverable in the contradictory elements of any received value mix.

Intrarealm Scarcity of Resources Implies Competition

Adequate resources allocated according to the wishes and desires of powerful actors seldom exist within any realm. Because the supply of laws, dollars, facilities, and personnel is almost always limited, the scarcity that develops is likely to lead to patterns of conflict and cooperation over resource allocation. Such conflicts and agreements which alter policy outcomes of the state are manifestly political and obviously are a source of policy.

The marijuana case is useful in illustrating this reasonably obvious proposition. The range of drugs categorized as dangerous defines one way of organizing the effort for their suppression. Marijuana, heroin, cocaine, and the new organic and synthetic hallucinogenic drugs each have distinctive patterns for their manufacture, importation, and distribution. Thus, resources devoted to the suppression of heroin may involve reductions in an antimarijuana campaign. To allocate resources differentially is by inference a value-structuring exercise which generates conflict between powerful actors who are for one reason or another tied to the removal of a particular drug from society.

Until quite recently, for instance, heroin use was for all practical purposes a problem of black urban populations. Marijuana use had "graduated" from blacks and Latins in the 1930s to entertainers and "bohemians" in the 1940s and 1950s. The great jump in popularity came in the middle of the 1960s when white college and high school students began to experiment with the drug in large numbers. By 1970 it was well known that heroin was psychologically and physiologically addictive and that it could be lethal. Moreover, there was widespread belief that heroin addiction was becoming highly associated with burglaries, holdups, and muggings in urban centers.

Dollars spent on enforcing the drug laws multiplied greatly during the 1960s, but the question of allocating these new resources was not simply answered by describing which drugs caused the worst social ills. Rather, it is highly likely that under conditions of scarcity, patterns of cooperation and conflict which evolved over time regarding each office's "share" determined how new resources were to be allocated.

Intrarealm conflict as a generator of policy change is better exemplified by the long-standing rivalries among the Army, Navy, and Air Force than by the marijuana issue. This classic pattern of intrarealm conflict should be noted as a case in which the conflict, while fueled by recurring issues, has *itself* become part of the received value mix of the individual services and their constituency and clientele networks. This intrarealm conflict has become institutionalized and stems from classic competition over the allocation of scarce public resources. Cooperative strategies between the services can be seen when the entire military portion of the budget comes into question. At that point the received value mix suggests the kinds of cooperation and joint efforts likely to be made in order to successfully compete with other realms. Unlike the marijuana case, the matter of interservice rivalry seems to have slowly evolved into part of the received value mix of the politics of national defense.

Scarce Public Resources Imply Competition Between Realms

If one grants the notion that politics involves conflict and cooperation between powerful actors over scarce public resources, then it follows that interrealm politics are likely to be significant. Competition and cooperation are best understood at the interrealm level as approximating a peculiar form of market. A number of actors compete for the valuable resources of legal monopoly, funds, constituency networks, and personnel. The marijuana case provides a less than perfect example of this sort of politics.

Anslinger and the Bureau of Narcotics operated within an ever more complicated area of public policy. The Treasury Department, the Justice Department, and the Public Health Service provided the organizational setting for conflict at the national level. State and local programs for enforcement and for treatment of drug cases provided yet another set of foci for the allocative process. In addition, powerful agencies at every level contained constituency networks concerned with law enforcement and social services in general. Realms involved with deviance *in general* were likely sources of support or of potential threats to an agency that dominated any specific area of social control.

Anslinger managed to maintain sufficient control over the delicate "foreign relations" between agencies for many years. His "narcs" cooperated with and assisted FBI personnel, so that a relationship of mutual benefit and exchange endured for years between obviously potential competitors. As long as marijuana remained a "threat" confined to a rather specific population and as long as the Bureau of Narcotics grew incrementally and not at the apparent expense of any of its potential competitors, Anslinger could maintain a virtual monopoly over public policy in this area under the Marijuana Tax Act of 1937 and subsequent legislation which he helped to author. Change elements eventually became activated for a variety of reasons, the most significant of which is identified below as a fourth source of policy. Before I proceed to discuss that source, it must be emphasized that the change in marijuana policy which we seem to be in the midst of could just as well have been generated from interrealm conflict earlier in the game if, for instance, HEW actors had been aggressively seeking new problems to include in the ever-expanding universe of problems that they have successfully defined as their own.

Structural Changes in the Environment Imply Subsequent Alterations in Policy

In chapter one it was suggested that beyond the purely governmental one had to look to constituent actors representing either large and/or powerful groups in society as a key source of policy change. This claim still stands, but it requires elaboration and amendment under the particular conditions discussed below.

A structural change in the environment is one that involves many members of the society who by their behavior bring about an alteration in the generally received value mix by creating a new zone of conflict. Such structural change is usually slow and is often comprehended by the appropriate political realm long after it has taken place. Occasionally, structural characteristics of the social order are simply unnoticed or ignored at the peril of some realm of state legitimacy. Prohibition serves as the usual example of the capacity of political actors to fail to notice a structural aspect of society. People drank before, during, and after the existence of the Eighteenth Amendment to the Constitution. That monument to old-fashioned pressure-group politics can provide us with some useful insights into the questions of enforceability, structural change in the environment, and the capacity of agencies of the state to alter aspects of the social order.

Prohibition is in some important ways parallel to the marijuana case. The Eighteenth Amendment came into existence through the persistence of a long-standing, highly active cluster of pressure groups. The foci of the successful Prohibitionists were the state legislatures whose votes were needed for ratification. Once the Amendment was ratified, the federal government, specifically the Treasury Department, undertook the enforcement role. What did they face? They were charged with the responsibility of forbidding any citizen to engage in a "crime without a victim." Millions of people did not believe buying a drink to be either sinful or even mildly criminal. The key to the prohibition problem was really a failure to recognize an aspect of the social order which was discoverable in every class, occupation, racial, and ethnic group. This much could have been readily observed in the process of altering the Constitution to proscribe an individual act that was alleged to have serious collective consequences.

The first lesson to be learned from the disaster of prohibition is that there are limits to what the state may do which have nothing whatever to do with law, but which arise instead from custom. Such limits usually are not apparent until some foolish act of the state brings them to widespread notice. Those who claimed that effective prohibition would not constitute a major structural alteration in the social order failed to perceive the situation correctly. Those who guessed that people did indeed wish to drink but who argued that the state had a higher moral obligation requiring forceful alteration of that wish were to discover the limits of state power, as it quickly became apparent that the costs of enforcing the law were prohibitive in the face of widespread disobedience. The story does not end there, however, because repeal of the Eighteenth Amendment is at least as interesting as its enactment.

Repeal, to shorten a long story unfairly, occurred as powerful actors came to realize that structural changes in the society negated the policy of prohibition which had unfortunately been codified in the Constitution. I say "unfortunately" because the Constitution is one of those vital symbols that is manipulated to achieve compliance. Such manipulation cannot be trivialized in a society which so values law and practically deifies the Constitution. Confrontations between the Constitution and widespread social custom have a deleterious effect on the rule of law. The social order did change as a result of prohibition, but repeal did not simply restore a *status quo ante* for tipplers.

Another important lesson about the role of structural change in the environment in terms of subsequent alterations in policy can be learned from the prohibition case. Not only did large numbers of citizens become lawbreakers by virtue of buying a drink, but wholesale changes in the nature of crime were stimulated by state action. The Eighteenth Amendment was, pardon the pun, the godfather of organized crime in the United States. This is not to say that it caused organized crime to develop. It merely turned millions of citizens into actual and potential consumers of illegal goods in the form of wine, whiskey, and beer. The importation, manufacture, financing, and distribution of intoxicants grew in classic capitalist fashion. Thus, prohibition contributed to the creation of a systemic blight that has cost lives and billions of dollars. Social customs changed. Adolescence in America was altered not only by the rumble seat but by the possibility of access to the speakeasy, one of the crowning achievements of prohibition's capacity to give birth to multifunctional social institutions. For a young person to enter a speakeasy for the first time constituted a "rite of passage" into adulthood in America in the 1920s. To be the godfather of organized crime was to be the creator of routes of upward economic and, eventually, social mobility for thousands of people for whom the conventional routes were unavailable.

Prohibition became the central law enforcement problem of the nation and generated bureaucratic growth and elaboration throughout the system in response to public reaction to the law. Organized crime and the powerful federal presence in law enforcement remain long after the great bootleggers have disappeared. Public policy and the received value mix characterizing much of the law enforcement realm today were thus heavily influenced by structural alterations in the environment *engendered in part by prohibition*. The state altered social structure in an unanticipated manner and is still evolving policies directed at certain aspects of the environment that *it helped to create*. One does not need an elaborate theory of society to begin to comprehend the effects that prohibition had on the received value mixes of the law enforcement realm or on organized crime. The marijuana case has some obvious similarities and differences that help to illuminate some of the ways in which structural changes in the environment seem to imply subsequent alterations in policy.

As suggested above, the act of defining something as political has great potential significance, particularly when the winner of a struggle to define the political in some realm is a bureaucratic actor. Clearly, Anslinger was victorious in defining marijuana as political through his formulation of national legislative and administrative drug policy. He was also very successful in influencing state legislatures to adopt substantially similar policies. This success rested on altering the received value mix of these realms to include marijuana in their catalog of social evils. A potential client and victim population was also created. To a great extent this population consisted of people who might ordinarily be classified as clients or victims for other purposes. Blacks, Latins, and juvenile delinquents were already receiving attention from the formally organized agents of social control for a variety of reasons. Marijuana use became simply another deviant act to be removed from this general population.

Slowly at first, then with greater and greater velocity, the drug began to become popular with more and more people. As suggested above, jazz musicians, "bohemians," then "beatniks," and, finally, "hippies" became associated with the drug. Users were apprehended, tried, and often sentenced to prison terms equal to those meted out for violent crimes. The "problem," as most people know, developed when the routinized arrest, prosecution, and conviction process began to involve the sons and daughters of the middle classes. Large numbers of kids from "good" homes began smoking marijuana.[5] Arrests with the potential of long prison sentences began to seem curiously unjust to many people. Still, law enforcement agencies maintained marijuana suppression in its by-now familiar position in the received value mix of their realm. Soon doctors, lawyers, other professionals, and white-collar workers with jobs, families, and all the trappings of respectability began smoking the noxious weed. The pattern of their use was hardly likely to be furtive "tokes" in back alleys or in smoky dorm rooms whose doors were insulated from sneaky deans by stuffing towels under them. Nice ladies at sophisticated parties passed the stuff around like martinis. Such people didn't seem to become murderers or rapists.

The proportions of this change in the use and users of marijuana are still not known for sure. Tens of millions of occasional and frequent users are believed by government agencies to be in society. If marijuana is to become the "new prohibition," then we may expect that policy will eventually adjust to this structural change. The laws prohibiting its use are for all practical purposes unenforceable. A variety of alternative strategies are at the moment being proposed for the coming removal or redefinition of marijuana in the received value mix of those realms concerned with the drug.

Marijuana is now a public health concern as well as a criminal justice matter. Localities and states have begun to ignore its use, "decriminalize" it, or are in the process of adjusting in some other ways to the fact that the population of users has begun to be identified by themselves and others as not criminal. We are in a transitional phase, one in which structural change in the greater society has altered the behaviors of political actors who through politics are altering the received value mix. The political structure of marijuana enforcement is thus in the process of fundamental change after nearly forty years of relative stasis and incremental growth based on outdated assumptions.

[5] In 1972 the Shafer Commission, which produced the *Report* that so upset President Nixon, claimed that 24,000,000 Americans had tried the drug at least once. The Commission's study found that 39% of young adults (18–25) had tried marijuana. These figures may be found on p. 7 of the *Report*.

Moral, scientific, administrative, and political value mixes which were received and which looked to be cemented as political structure will change because the social order has altered seriously as to the structure of marijuana use. This source of policy change is as interesting as it is unusual. There are few easy examples of such widespread and rapid alterations in public behavior which in its aggregate effects imply the necessity of policy change. The alteration is likely to be explained by elaborate scientific research. The crux of the matter is that when laws become unenforceable because many people believe their violation insignificant, then policy will change. Widespread disobedience diminishes the power of the state which rests on the expectation of acceptance of the outcomes of politics by citizens, constituents, clients, and victims.

A note of caution must conclude this discussion of structural changes in the environment as implying subsequent alterations in policies. The social order, which is the general "environment" of the political system, is always in a state of change. Seldom do changes occur throughout all strata of society as appears to be the case with marijuana use. The marijuana example and the prohibition case are unusual for this reason and by virtue of the fact that both matters involve personal acts which directly confront that most obvious manifestation of state power, the criminal justice system. Structural changes in society which are of great import do not necessarily become political issues through noncompliant acts. Rather, changes in social behavior significant enough to be called structural are likely to be the stuff of constituency–bureaucracy resource mobilization which results in intrarealm and extrarealm competition over the allocation of scarce public resources.

The Scheme of Analysis: Recapitulation and Synthesis

This seems an appropriate point to pause for a brief recapitulation of the major concepts presented thus far. It will also be useful to briefly describe their interrelationships. The five major concepts are:

1. *Politics:* Conflict and cooperation over scarce public resources, including definitions of the political and its realms.
2. *Received value mixes:* Policies embodied in the laws, rules, customs, beliefs, and desires which have regulated and directed agencies of the state and their constituent and clientele networks over time. These

mixes are political structure and serve to mark the realms of the political.

3. *Political realms:* Those places in time and space where politics takes place. Realms of the political are defined and redefined by changes in the received value mix which are often associated with changing the previously "apolitical" into the political. The realms of the political are most readily discovered in public agencies and their constituency and clientele networks.

4. *Policies:* The results of political conflict and cooperation which are discoverable in the form of laws, regulations, and changes in the allocative patterns of public resources.

5. *Policy change:* Four sources are identified as major:
   (a) Received value mixes imply conflict through contradiction.
   (b) Intrarealm scarcity of resources implies competition.
   (c) Scarce public resources imply competition between realms.
   (d) Structural changes in the environment imply subsequent alterations in policy.

Perhaps a single sentence will convey a synthesis of the analysis thus far and can also provide a basis for further elaboration of the conceptual framework. *Received value mixes* inhere in persons and institutions which define *realms* where *politics* create *policy* and *policy change.* This formulation points us in a direction which suggests that the general typification of political phenomena is likely to be a difficult task. A useful approach is to continue to talk of realms and of mixes. This we will do, but at the cost of transcendent analysis which might otherwise have proven useful. The exception to this stricture follows immediately upon its injunction. I proceed to this exception because it aids in the analysis, and I believe it to contain propositions which vitally underpin contemporary political life.

The General Roots of Political Demand

The Weberian Formulation of the State and Society

Max Weber wrote the following in his famous essay "On Bureaucracy":[6]

[6] Hans H. Gerth and C. Wright Mills, eds., *From Max Weber* (New York: Oxford University Press, 1958), pp. 212–213.

. . . The growing demands on culture, in turn, are determined, though to a varying extent, by the growing wealth of the most influential strata in the state. To this extent increasing bureaucratization is a function of the increasing possession of goods used for consumption, and of an increasingly sophisticated technique of fashioning external life—a technique which corresponds to the opportunities provided by such wealth. This reacts upon the standard of living and makes for an increasing subjective indispensability of organized, collective, interlocal, and thus bureaucratic, provision for the most varied wants, which previously were either unknown, or were satisfied locally or by a private economy.

Weber's points are much more pertinent now than when he made them nearly three generations ago. It is my intention to elucidate his meaning and to expand the concept of subjective indispensability beyond that meaning in order to enrich the conceptual framework and analysis which I have been developing. In the passage quoted above Weber notes that not only is bureaucracy likely to flourish in a social system in which wealth is not equally diffused, but he also suggests that demand itself is stimulated by bureaucracy. Given an expanding money economy and an unequal distribution of wealth, Weber argues that bureaucracy itself becomes a generator of "increasing subjective indispensability." He is explicit about the *collective, subjective,* and *previously unknown* character of such *wants.*

In the above passage Weber draws attention to the citizen as a recipient of goods and services from bureaucracies which could not be produced by smaller-scale organizations or private economies. This observation may be summarized as an "economy of scale explanation" for the bureaucratic phenomenon. Thus, the unit costs of goods and services are supposed to decline as an increased division of labor in their production increases. A concomitant increase in demand is essential to effectively keep unit costs to the manufacturer and consumer lower than what they had been.

But Weber has much more to say than this. He says that, given economic and social stratification, ". . . increasing possession of goods used for consumption . . . and increasingly sophisticated techniques for fashioning external life . . ." become functionally related to increased bureaucratization. I read "the techniques for fashioning external life" to mean technological systems associated with social and economic life. The man–machine technologies developing before Weber's eyes *seemed* to be creating organizational structures for their management and for the distribution of their produce. Weber believed that these structures (bureaucracies) were long in development but had reached fruition in the rush of nineteenth-century industrialization. He further believed that the bureaucratization of economic, political, and social life was imminent, inevitable, and had the most profound significance for civilization. Weber urges us to attend to the implications of physical technologies, organizational technologies, and the environment which seems necessary to bring them into existence and to sustain them once they are fully established.

Weber thought that state bureaucracy was an essential tool for the development of modern economic systems through the creation of infrastructure in the form of publicly incubated and administered transportation and communication networks. He also believed that the modern state itself could not come into being and could not sustain itself without bureaucratic organization. Social, economic, and political control could be firmly established only by the routinized and authoritative administration of public policy that his model of bureaucracy described. Weber's was an essentially developmental argument which had at its core an assumption that certain requisites of control had to be established in order for the modern state to exist. Economic infrastructure creation and its public administration was one of these requisites. Absolute pacification through the establishment of bureaucratic systems of justice was another "requisite" as was a policy of social welfare. The latter is akin to the "police power" in the American states in that it had to do with the health, safety, and welfare of the public.[7]

For Weber the state was that unique entity which exercised legitimate control over force and coercion through law. It did so, he believed, most fairly, impartially, and successfully through the creation of bureaucratic structure. Thus, the development of modern economies and the stability of the state rests, in Weber's view, on that instrument of power without parallel, the bureaucracy. In this form of rigid, hierarchical, specialized structure which was so terribly effective in coordinating development and regulating behavior there lurked a series of major contradictions. One of these involved the general question of persons-within-organizations, a contradiction which has been the subject of debate among managers, social scientists, literary people, and public administrationists for decades. This contradiction is beyond the scope of immediate

[7] This summary of Weber's thought and the discussion that follows are my interpretation, drawn from his "On Bureaucracy" (Gerth and Mills, eds., *From Max Weber*) and from his *Theory of Social and Economic Organization,* Talcott Parsons, ed. and trans. by A. M. Henderson (New York: The Free Press, 1964).

analysis and will be touched on only briefly in subsequent chapters. The other major contradiction is a central concern of this book and has to do with the generation of subjective indispensability.

Weber argues that as bureaucratization of the state proceeds as a partial function of increased wealth in the "influential strata," a new set of social circumstances pertains. Specifically, there is an increase in the goods used for consumption and an increase in the technologies employed in their production. In short, increased consumption by the upper strata yields sufficient accumulated profit for investment in ever more complex technologies for the manufacture of such goods. Furthermore, this growth can proceed only when the state creates, controls, and directs certain fundamental aspects of social life, enumerated above as "requisites" (the term is mine or Talcott Parsons, *not* Weber's). This process leads to a division of individual and collective labor which makes local production and consumption of many goods and services impossible. This is so because people begin to work in highly specialized roles which prevent them from having time to do various other tasks necessary for their existence (such as growing their own food). People also can purchase goods and services less expensively from large organizations than they can if they produce them themselves or buy them from economically inefficient local producers. This broad formulation leads to the logical necessity of a ready means of transportation and communication for labor, materials, and products. It also leads us back to a social environment with a minimum of civil strife and banditry, thus enabling the great engine of industrialization to proceed. Social disorder of any sort must be dealt with lest it interrupt economic development, and so Weber posits the social welfare and absolute pacification requisites.[8]

The Conversion of Wants into Needs

The contradiction arises when, as Weber points out, this process "reacts upon the standard of living." I interpret Weber to mean than an increased propensity to consume is transmitted throughout the strata of society. Two things happen. First, people must have their needs for food, fiber, and shelter met by bureaucratic organizations or by organizations locally dependent upon some central agency. These needs are at this

[8] He does this on p. 213, Gerth and Mills, eds., *From Max Weber*.

stage of analysis "purely" economic (insofar as anything may be said to be purely economic). The division of labor alone requires it to be so. People depend upon *national* institutions, corporations, markets, and governments even in the relatively primitive stages of industrial development. I expand on Weber when I suggest that *growing interdependence arising out of a technologically energized division of labor makes individual and even local community self-dependence an impossibility.* Failure of the state to support this situation becomes an immediate precondition for chaos, depression, and/or revolution. Since this condition of interdependence grows, the state activities that support and regulate it must also grow. The form of this growth may be broadly characterized as bureaucratic.

The situation becomes even more complex when one considers the question of indispensability. I begin with the matter of the conversion of wants into needs. Wants become converted to needs in two ways. At that moment in history when one's desire to have a telephone because it makes life easier is translated into a necessity for existence in a civilized world, a conversion occurs which can be objectively accounted for. One either needs a phone to conduct one's life, or one does not. If one cannot earn a living without a phone, he needs the thing. If one cannot receive emergency assistance without a telephone, then he needs the thing (particularly if his house is afire). The want of the phone over time becomes the need as complex interdependence increases. In our era the absence of widely diffused, highly integrated communication systems is literally impossible to imagine. My grandfather's want became my father's need. How many other wants became *objectively verifiable* needs in that short span between one's grandfather's adulthood and one's own? Thousands of examples could probably be supplied for those who live in urbanized and suburbanized societies. One could argue long about the objectively verifiable nature of some needs of urbanized humanity, but that argument would begin in most cases with an enormous quantity of mutually agreed upon needs unimagined by one's grandfather or even by Max Weber.[9]

[9] Technological and scientific advances diffused through complex economic and organizational means become objectively indispensable as well as objectively verifiable in many ways. For example, if one assumes that people prefer life over death, the objectively verifiable need for a cure becomes evident when one has a potentially lethal bacterial infection. Prior to the discovery of and widespread availability of antibiotics such a sick person had an objectively verifiable need but no possibility of its satisfaction. Now that antibiotics are available, the patient's objectively verifiable need makes the drugs objectively indispensable.

The appearance of what has been identified as "objectively verifiable" needs in ever increasing numbers is a partial explanation for the growth of the modern state. If one grants the existence of accelerating governmental provision of services to meet these needs through large-scale, formal organizations, then one is on the road to explaining the bureaucratic state. Weber argued that bureaucracy as a *form* or organization was an incomparable, neutral instrument, capable of accumulating, organizing, and distributing resources. In meeting demand in the form of wants converted to needs, state bureaucracy also managed to contribute to the generation of new demands.

The distribution of governmental services creates inequity through the division of labor and because all members of the society seldom benefit equally from all public actions. A new road to village X may be constructed at the cost of a new road to village Y. Furthermore, the new road to Y may be more "rational" than the one to X, but the folks in X are more influential in the political process that creates new roads. Specialization of governmental function benefits some persons more than others, and politics always involves allocation of scarce public resources, favoring some over others. Weber would probably be unhappy with this formulation, but I believe it to be a reasonable inference from his analysis.

Not only do most actions of the state differentially benefit some segments of society. The unequal distribution of wealth stemming from industrialization creates even more serious cleavages. These two elements of cleavage, when added to the class and ethnic status differences in nineteenth-century Prussia, led Weber to formulate an hypothesis which he partially states in the quotation above. That is, as economic development proceeds to involve more and different individual consumption, people find themselves both needful *and* desirous of more and different goods and services. One of the major sources of such goods and services is the state.

Desires become collective, subjective, and previously unknown. As these wants become common attributes of collectivities, they become "subjectively indispensable." Thus, government action generates not only demand for more of the existing services and for equity in their distribution, but government may also cause people to convert wants into needs where none existed before.

This is an expansion of the Weberian formulation and may be illustrated in contemporary settings without great strain. If, for instance, one lives in an economically distressed area, one might attempt to improve conditions by trying to get the Air Force to build a base locally. Air Force officials might concede that the local economy would gain a considerable boost if a base were to be constructed, but they may see no military reason to do so. If, however, one's congressman happens to be the chairman of the House Armed Services Committee, then the likelihood of the Air Force's altering its position increases somewhat. Some kind of installation will probably be constructed. This is not an uncommon formulation of one of the routines of American politics. The point, however, is that the political actors involved represent their case in terms of *subjective* (there is, we assume, no reason to build the facility in this district, if indeed there is any need to build the thing at all) *indispensability*. There is a desire to boost the local economy, and an agency of the state becomes (to the actors involved) indispensable to the achievement of that want which has become a need.

That the state has become the source of potential economic recovery for this fictional area is not an issue today. That the Air Force should be the means of implementing this transformation is hardly an imaginative thought. Furthermore, if private sector economic interests were to find this district attractive, then the claim on the Air Force might be lessened. But since we have tacitly assumed that private sector business is unwilling to locate in the area, people believe it indeed subjectively indispensable for the state to fill the role that was filled by the local economy or which was previously unfulfilled. The state filled no such role deliberately fifty years ago. That millions of persons now believe the state ought to stimulate local economies through its administrative agencies is a value which seems reasonably set. It is set in the received value mixes of Rotarians and poverty workers, computer programmers and janitors, Republicans and Democrats.

Deprivations of birth, situation, economic well-being, and nearly every aspect of the human condition have become the business of government. As prescient as Weber was, he could not have imagined the extent to which the "subjective indispensability of organized, collective, previously unknown and varied wants" have become the focus of state action. Injustice and inequity in nearly all aspects of existence have become "problems" which political actors believe to be within the realm of state "solutions."

When modern states began to satisfy objectively indispensable needs, they aided in the stimulation of subjectively indispensable wants. The state and the economy which underpins it have become objects of steadily rising expectations and of massive relative deprivation. Expectations of the disadvantaged and the relatively deprived have become the sum and substance of much political activity in the bureaucratic state. I am relatively deprived if my place of residence prevents me from acquiring an education equal to that of my neighbor who attends a better school. True, I receive a "free" public education, but not as good a one as my neighbor does. I am thus relatively deprived. The absence of *any* educational opportunity constitutes absolute deprivation. Rising expectations and relative deprivation are created when the state forms educational systems that vary in quality.

I differentiate objective and subjective indispensability on the arbitrary grounds of minimal necessity for the maintenance of life. But this is clearly a distinction that is arguable in the extreme. I choose to let it remain so, because I have no "answer" to where the line is to be drawn, and more importantly, because the question of objective and subjective indispensability *is precisely one of those crucial acts of defining the political and its realm.* We know that complex interdependence grows and that this necessarily converts wants into needs. Indeed, we can suggest that as economic and political life becomes more highly differentiated and productive under what appears to be a technological imperative which used to be called progress, personal and institutional interdependence increases. New wants and new needs are *created,* as are new dependencies and new relative and absolute deprivations.

The capacity of powerful political actors to authoritatively define one or more aspects of demand relevant to some significant population becomes a crucial question. Alterations in the received value mix of any political realm become in part a function of constituency mobilization or creation. Subjective and objective indispensability, as reformulated from Weber, are convenient categories for typifying general phenomena in the society. But as I have suggested repeatedly, such generalizations are of little utility unless we examine the variety of ways in which demand within political realms becomes recognized, acted upon, and eventually institutionalized. This I shall attempt to exemplify in the following chapters, because different histories, ideologies, and institutions characterize different political realms.

The general roots of demand discussed thus far constitute the rumbling pressure of the social order in which the state is embedded. Our separation of the state from its environment is in part an analytical conceit and necessity. The state is so inextricably involved in modern life that we lack a modern philosophical conception of it. The concepts outlined and developed above stem from a desire to understand how it is that we appear to be a nation of citizens who are constituents, clients, and victims.

Conclusions

The framework for analysis stems from the initial question posed at the end of chapter one. It will be recalled that the problem of explaining or accounting for the observations in that chapter involved the formulation of a conceptual framework. A framework has been developed that attempts to provide some analytical concepts to aid in understanding the American political world in terms of the claimed centrality of public agencies.

To repeat: *Received value mixes* inhere in persons and institutions which define *realms* in which *politics* create *policy* and *policy change*. The social fuel that generally energizes policy change was identified specifically as having four major sources, the last of which (the implication of policy change as a function of structural changes in the environment) involved a more lengthy discussion of some concepts of demand. This extrapolation and extension of some of the thought of Max Weber was concerned with some general formulations. These may be briefly summarized as follows. Growing economic interdependence involves the generation of needs for increased state intervention in the early stages of industrialization. Animated by a vastly increasing division of labor, characterized by increasingly complex mechanical and organizational technologies, personal and institutional wants and needs have become more numerous and varied. Goods and services desired by all strata of society have become converted into needs. These needs I arbitrarily divided into "objective" and "subjective" indispensabilities. The former is said to be discoverable as a function of complex interdependence and the latter by relative deprivation and rising expectation.

In this general statement I attempted to broadly characterize what I believe to be some of the major sources of demand within the environment of the state. I will attempt to illustrate some aspects of these concepts of demand in the following chapters, but my primary focus will be on political realms and received value mixes. If the concepts of political realms and of received value mixes are to be useful analytical tools, then they must be applied to empirical settings for purposes of illustration and elucidation.

The three chapters that follow are therefore dedicated to this task. Since I have argued that the received value mixes of political realms change over time and differ among themselves, I will attempt to illustrate the truth of that observation and the propositions which underpin it by applying this framework to three areas of public policy which are generally conceded to be significant aspects of American political life.

An important qualification must be stated at this point. The analysis of the three major realms of political life in chapters three, four, and five is not intended to be comprehensive or substantively penetrating. The analysis is intended to be heuristic and illustrative. It is grounded in the questions raised by the concepts described in the framework presented. My purpose is, therefore, to illustrate the utility of that framework and to expand upon it as each political realm is discussed.

In each instance I will deal with the received value mix of the realm as it developed over time and as it defined the political. I will attempt to describe and analyze the politics and processes of policy generation and change that characterize each realm, especially in terms of evolving bureaucratic organization. Emphasis will also be placed on accounting for the differing value mixes within the realms. Special attention will be paid to the evolving significance of mechanical and organizational technologies. The organizational entities and policies contained within these realms will finally be analyzed in terms of the significant constituent, client, and victim populations associated with them.

chapter three

The Realm
of Political Economy

The relationship of the state to the economy is one of the enduring themes of American history. This analysis of the realm of political economy traces some aspects of that relationship. The argument in the following pages holds that the realm has been dominated by constituency relationships in the formation of public policy.

The central actors in the realm at the end of the last century were legislatures, courts, and those evolving concentrations of economic power, the trusts, created out of corporate organization. In the present century constituency relationships changed when the expanded and elaborated public bureaucracy became the focus of more and different kinds of economic interests. Large, complex economic organizations became interactive and interdependent with the state over time, such that a reformulated notion of bureaucratic constituency now characterizes the realm.

The first century of American economic history provided certain general values that still survive as active elements of the contemporary received mix. At the risk of dangerous exclusion, let me summarize these as stimulation, support, and laissez faire individualism. The legacy of this era lies in our current belief that it is right and proper for government to *stimulate* economic growth and development through the construction of public works as well as through other devices which are understood to be strictly governmental responsibilities.

Support for private enterprise also became embedded in the received mix of the industrializing economy, although this value has a curious duality about it. Direct subsidy of certain enterprises was permissible through land grants to railroads, farmers, and those in the business of extracting minerals from the earth. In some cases, even cash grants were permissible if one could successfully invoke "public need" through manipulation of the political process. At the same time we are recipients of a value which indicates that support must not involve the competition of government enterprise with private enterprise. This duality, which is in effect a contradiction, exists because of the third value, *laissez faire individualism.*

This latter component of the received value mix suggests that in economic affairs that government is best which governs least. People left to their own devices ought to be able to construct a more productive economy. Unrestrained by government, people will participate in the marketplace to maximize personal gain, and the structures they thereby create will benefit others. Factories create jobs when people sell their labor to the owners of the factories. The profit earned by the manufacturer and the wages earned by the laborer create disposable wealth that can then be used for investment, thus creating more factories, more jobs, and so on.

Capitalism, unrestrained but supported and stimulated by the state, was by 1887 part of the received value mix of those realms of the political that dealt with the relationship of government to economy. I believe that this legacy is still to be discovered in the present era, and that it limits, directs, and animates contemporary politico-economic realms and the processes of policy formulation and generation that typify them.

To the values of *stimulation, support,* and *laissez faire individualism,* the value of *regulation for expansion* was added during the period 1887–1933. The creations of those who wished to turn government regulation toward a concern for the public interest and a more equitable distribution of benefits ironically served a different purpose. The regulatory agency provided an unrivaled opportunity for the institutionalization of private economic interest *within* the corpus of the state. The realms of the political underwent a serious change during this period. Legislatures lost through delegation much of the effective power to intervene in the activities of the private sector. Powerful industrial and commercial interests at first did battle with attempts at regulation. Eventually, they realized that political power could be wielded very effectively by co-opting the regulatory process. Bribes, political contributions, and propaganda, while not entirely disappearing from the scene, became less appropriate as it became clear that many of the important day-to-day operations of the state relevant to specific economic interests were to be discovered outside the legislative arena.

The received value mix as of 1933 was a cluster of policies that tended to define the economic realm in contradictory and confusing ways. Laissez faire individualism and regulation for expansion seem at first to be the most seriously contradictory elements of the realm as defined thus far. In practice, however, the contradiction was submerged and obscured by the conversion of regulatory agencies to legitimated representatives of private sector interest. Thus, by 1933 the Department of Agriculture had long been a creature of organized farmers and their friends in Congress. The Interstate Commerce Commission was a preserve of the railroads. The received value mix was altered during this era by the creation of structures of regulation that rapidly became dominated by the very industries and interests that they had been intended to regulate; private sector interests jumped into the beds created for them by the state. The process was discontinuous and incremental, as it has always been in American politics. By 1933 the industrial state consisted of a series of legitimated satrapies dominated by private actors. The aggregate effects of this domination were unknown. The powers of the state were diffused, diluted, and often turned to the direct benefit of the specialized interests of the industrial and commercial world.

America on the Eve of Economic Crisis: A Summary Portrait—1933

It will be helpful to note some of the major structural changes in society and the economy that had accumulated to provide a setting for the great political drama that was to unfold. One hundred and forty years had elapsed between the time Washington got stuck in the Susquehanna[1] and the time that America got stuck in the Great Depression. In that very short period of time, thirteen colonies clinging to the eastern seaboard were transformed into a continental nation. The conquest of the physical environment, the fighting of a disastrous internal war, the absorption of

[1] The epitome of the great economic problems facing the new nation is reflected in the following quotation taken from Leonard D. White's classic administrative history of the United States, *The Federalists* (New York: Macmillan, 1948), p. 1.

On October 25, 1794, the President of the United States was returning from Bedford, Pennsylvania, to the seat of government. While crossing the Susquehanna River, his coach became lodged between two boulders in midstream, and he was forced to sit in the rain until it could be extricated.

millions of immigrants, the urbanization of the populace, the development of mechanical and organizational technologies, and the incredible expansion of wealth and consumption had never been equaled.

The physical conquest and settlement of the continental United States had been concluded within the memory of those who were middle-aged in 1933. The movement of the population was far from over, however. The drift from inefficient small farms to economically viable agri-businesses began in the last quarter of the nineteenth century and has continued ever since. People left the farm to go to the city, because the cities contained the wealth of the nation. There, farm boys could find steady labor in factories and mills. As much of our urbanization can be accounted for by internal migration from the hinterland as from foreign shores. The apex of foreign immigration was the period 1890–1914, during which the population nearly doubled. America in the 1920s was a Babel of foreign tongues and a haven for ambition.

As wealth increased, so too did consumption. Technological change and an unheard-of expansion of personal credit made possible the development of a new middle class, and slowly, but perceptibly, wealth trickled down to the army of wage earners. They were educated by the hundreds of thousands in free public educational institutions created by the state, and they assumed new roles in the expanding industrial system. Sales, marketing, accounting, and dozens of other functions *associated* with the production of goods and services created new jobs, new roles, and new organizational technologies.

Organizational technology is of particular interest. A brief digression illuminates and defines the meaning of an organizational technology, and, incidentally, tells us something about government participation in the economy. In 1851 the British held their famous Crystal Palace Exposition. The purpose of the exposition was to display the technological wonders of the day. The American contribution was a demonstration of the technology of manufacturing complex mechanisms that had interchangeable parts. The Americans showed that they could assemble devices with low error tolerances out of parts produced at different times and even at different places.

The British were so impressed with this "American System," as they called it, that they sent a parliamentary committee to investigate its use in the firearms industry. When they visited the U.S. armory at Springfield, Massachusetts, they discovered that a workman could assemble a working musket out of the disassembled parts of muskets produced over a ten-year span. Members of the committee handed the workman the parts and observed in wonder the ease and speed with which he assembled the weapon. The British bought not only the mechanical technology (the machines) from the Americans, but they also bought the idea of interchangeability (the organizational technology) and helped to diffuse it throughout the world.[2]

Two things are of interest in this little example. First, the government invested public capital to produce firearms for the armed forces, despite the fact that there were adequate private producers. This occurred in the middle of what some believe was a golden age of nonintervention. Second, the idea and the product were diffused without charge to the world. The prime significance lies in the design of a system that would be adapted by organizational pioneers in the century following the Crystal Palace Exposition.

On the eve of the Great Depression millions were riding about in their own automobiles, produced at an affordable price by a corporation dedicated to the lessons of the Springfield armory. By 1933 Americans expected technological change to be as significant an accelerator of economic expansion as the utilization of natural resources. Instead of an economy based simply on the classic factors of production (land, labor, and capital), a new resource was in the process of being recognized: the development of organizational and mechanical technologies through innovation. From invention to application to marketing and distribution, Americans lived in a new world of technological possibility. It was a world that had produced basic changes in their daily labor and probably in their whole existence.

The stock market crashed in 1929, and by 1933 millions of people were unemployed. They drove their Model T Fords past empty factories, they listened to the new President on the radio, and they turned their electric lights off to go to their worried beds. No one understood what had happened or why it had happened. The cars were sold or abandoned. Soon the houses went and the beds with them. The most vigorous population on earth turned from Babbittry to Depression.

2 This story is related in Lance E. Davis et al., *American Economic Growth* (New York: Harper & Row, 1972), p. 253.

Intervention for System Maintenance

The Democrats who took office in March of 1933 assumed the operation of an administrative structure that was fully geared to maintaining a system of economic expansion with minimal interference. Franklin D. Roosevelt was a child of the nineteenth century, steeped in the economic beliefs of his country and socialized to the received value mix of the realm of political economy. The problems he faced, however, were unprecedented. Unemployment, starvation, extreme social dislocation, and a seemingly moribund capitalism confronted his new administration. His unfairly reviled predecessor had tried all the means he believed to be at his disposal to counteract the disaster. There were no agencies of the state to deal with a crisis of this magnitude.

The regulatory commissions, the artifacts of system maintenance, the Congress, and the states seemed to have proven themselves inappropriate. The institution of the presidency was to emerge as a permanently significant actor in the realm of political economy. Roosevelt and his advisors evolved a strategy to combat the Depression which was a blend of political pragmatism and atheoretical interventionism. He quickly decided that emergency aid was needed in several key areas. Unemployment, bank failures, and the accompanying drop in aggregate demand were problems met by the federal government's becoming employer, banker, and consumer in ways and on a scale that had never been done before. Every sector of the economy was in trouble, and Roosevelt attacked the problems in a blaze of legislation and spending that was to have significant short-term and long-term effects.

State and local systems of welfare were predicated on nineteenth-century poorhouse legislation. The significant actors in social welfare during the period prior to the Roosevelt years were private charities. This structure of welfare was simply ignored, as were the urban machines. Harry Hopkins, who was for all practical purposes Roosevelt's assistant president, defined the political and its economic realm in dozens of actions too numerous to discuss here. A single example will convey some sense of how the realm of political economy was redefined and how the received value mix was significantly added to. Three and one-half weeks after he was appointed Federal Emergency Relief Administrator, Hopkins went to Detroit to make a speech. In that speech he stated that relief was an *obligation* of the federal government, that people had a *right* to cash payments instead of grocery store scrip, and that every American was *entitled* not only to food but also to medical care, clothing, and shelter.[3] He and his cohorts promised to meet these needs and to provide jobs as long as it should be necessary. Agency after agency was created to implement these goals. Element after element of the private sector became the direct concern of the Roosevelt administration.

Emergency relief soon gave way to more comprehensive and permanent structures of intervention. These structures, founded in crisis, have familiar historical names: NRA, CCC, AAA, PWA, WPA, and SEC.[4] The names are for the most part gone from our vocabulary, but some of the functions continue to be served in one organizational context or another. While the presidency was elevated to new significance in the realm of political economy, the implications of that elevation were even more profound. The state, through the creation of nationally significant public organizations, entered into a condition of permanent intervention. The activities and significance of public sector activity carried out by bureaucratic organizations were never to decline. Not only was regulation for expansion widened and deepened, but intervention for maintenance of the economic system also became a received value. The actors who brought this evolving system of regulation and intervention into existence could control it only during its infancy. As it matured, it became a nearly autonomous entity, sufficiently complex to be beyond even the immediate comprehension of its creators.

To conclude, the New Deal established large-scale national bureaucracies as new elements in the realm of political economy and permanently set the Office of the President as the single actor most politically responsible for the economic health of the nation. How this power was accumulated and consolidated into the received value mix involves some discussion of the politics of the era.

Roosevelt and his New Deal were believed by some to be traitorous to the received value of laissez faire individualism said to underpin not only the Horatio Alger myth[5] but also the very essence of capitalism itself. F.D.R. became convinced that in this time of crisis such beliefs were sufficiently submerged to permit his reorganizing the political

[3] For a detailed account of Hopkins and his exploits, see Robert E. Sherwood, *Roosevelt and Hopkins* (New York: Harper, 1948).

[4] National Recovery Administration, Civilian Conservation Corps, Agricultural Adjustment Act, Public Works Administration, Works Progress Administration, and Securities and Exchange Commission.

[5] Louis Hartz, *The Liberal Tradition in America* (New York: Harcourt, 1955). A brilliant account of the Alger motif in American political thought.

system by creating, defining, and recognizing functionally demarcated national constituencies.

Thus, the Wagner Act, establishing the National Labor Relations Board, brought the right of collective bargaining to unions and established them as a fixed star in the Democratic constellation and in the realm of political economy. The Social Security Act, guaranteeing pensions to retired workers, their widows, and those injured on the job, created *a constituency* of enormous electoral significance. Elaborate systems of farm price supports, mortgage guarantees, and rural electrification made new friends of farmers, small and large. Small bank depositors were encouraged to return to saving by federal insurance against bank failures. The politics of distribution and redistribution had begun with a vengeance, and those who looked to statehouses and urban bosses as countervailing sources of power were looking at dying artifacts of a bygone era.

Roosevelt's politics were based on clear perceptions of structural changes; these changes became evident only when the Depression thrust them into stark contrast with the received value mix of 1933. The first of these changes was that America was not a nation of small farmers and entrepreneurs; it was a nation of wage earners. Most of the labor force earned their wages in large industrial, commercial, or service enterprises.

The health of the national economy rested on the well-being of these enterprises and on the ability of their wage earners to consume. The age of advertising and of wide distribution of consumer goods had begun when the Depression struck.

Astute politicians (and there have been few as astute as F.D.R.) understood that the objective indispensabilities of food, fiber, and shelter had to be dealt with quickly, or widespread social dislocation might lead to unparalleled social unrest. The idea of revolution had occurred to more than just socialists and "reds." The fear of the bonus marchers, "Hoovervilles," and Steinbeck's Oakies, not to mention Communist unions and intellectuals, was real indeed. The Brain Trusters and many moderate Democrats and Republicans came to realize that there were some conditions that the general population could not long endure. Hunger, homelessness, and unemployment could not be tolerated beyond a certain level, if the social order was to remain stable. What the limit was, when actual revolt might occur—these questions no politician wanted to deal with.

Roosevelt's initial strategy was to bolster the provision of these objective indispensabilities through emergency measures. He, thus, can be understood as being profoundly conservative of the status quo, since he believed that the way to avoid massive social disintegration was to revitalize the received values in which he believed. The New Deal was not revolutionary in the sense that the term was applied to Russia in 1917. Indeed, the specter of the Soviet Union may have lain in the back of the minds of those who otherwise would not have given even tacit assent to New Deal programs.

Whether the New Deal "worked" or not is an interesting subject for discussion, but one we cannot raise in the detail it deserves. Suffice it to say that recurring recession in the late 1930s caused many to believe that the institutionalization of the New Deal into permanent structures of intervention was not *proven* to be effective. The point is that its functions became part of the received value mix, and the events of 1939–1946 make the question truly an academic one anyway.

The historic occasion that "ended" the Depression was, of course, World War II. The war and the mobilization of economic resources needed to win it were immediate contingencies when Roosevelt decided to run for a third term. By late afternoon on December 7, 1941, the debate over our possible involvement in hostilities was ended, and the New Dealers were once again involved in a crisis of vast magnitude. America was to become the "arsenal of democracy,"[6] and not a soul on the face of the earth could imagine what the ramifications of that were to be. Neither Roosevelt, Hopkins, nor the leaders of the armed forces of this nation, its allies, or enemies imagined the resource mobilization that was to come in the three years following the disaster at Pearl Harbor. The federal government was utterly unprepared for war in 1940. The armed forces had been kept at a subsistence level since 1918. As late as mid-1940 no one believed America could be in a two-front war, requiring the total mobilization and redirection of the private sector.

Roosevelt established the parent agencies for war production, manpower, price control, food production, and transportation before December 7, without authorization from Congress. He did this by using ancient statutes from the Civil War and raised the Selective Service issue only because he knew he had to. The presidency had become the crucial political force to mobilize the wartime economy. Executives came to Washington by the thousands and manned the bureaucracy of war production. The job of coordinating millions of laborers, thousands of

[6] This is the title of a book detailing the mobilization effort by a man who was one of its principal organizers. Donald Nelson, *Arsenal of Democracy* (New York: Harcourt, 1946).

producers, and the incredible complexity of transportation around the globe was essentially *improvised*[7] by creating large, new complex organizations which intervened into every aspect of the private sector. Thousands of committees, boards, hierarchies, and councils were set up in Washington and throughout the nation. Nothing quite like it had ever existed before, and one would have expected delays and, to use a term coined at the time, *snafus* (situation normal, all fouled up). There were plenty of the latter, but one cold empirical fact became obvious by 1945.

In three years the United States converted a peacetime economy into the most potent industrial force for military production in the history of the world. The Germans, the Japanese, the Russians, the Italians, and the British together did not produce in ten years what the Americans produced in three.[8] All the combatants had been in some state of preparation by 1941; all were industrial nations.

What can account for the utter defeat of the Axis powers in such a short period? Volumes of military and diplomatic explanation have been provided. I believe part of any explanation must consider the evolution of the realm of political economy. World War II proved that America had a national economy that could be centrally planned and directed. The agencies of planning, coordination, and direction were "quasi-public" in that they were well integrated *cooperatively* with the elites of the large enterprises that dominated the economy. Thus, intervention for the survival of the social order took place in the 1930s, while intervention for the survival of the world took place in the 1940s. The war was not just an unusual episode. It was the redirected continuation of what had begun in 1933. The state and the economy were shown to be highly complex, interrelated systems.

A Received Value Mix: 1946

Stimulation and *support, laissez faire individualism, regulation for expansion*—all of these elements remained in the received value mix in 1946. To these values was added *intervention for system maintenance*

---

[7] Much of the initial framework of wartime industrial organization derived from World War I experience. That framework was, I believe, transformed so thoroughly that by 1945 a whole new pattern of relationships between government and industry had emerged. See Nelson, *Arsenal of Democracy*.

[8] Albert Speer, *Inside the Third Reich* (New York: Avon, 1970).

during the tumultuous years of the Roosevelt administration. An important New Deal contribution to the received value mix can be summarized in a single statement: *The market was never again to be trusted as the sole determinant of the economic well-being of the nation.* The near-catastrophic failure of the market to maintain equilibrium led the way to the creation of mechanisms and institutions of permanent intervention. Never again would the market be allowed to be anything other than a mixture of public and private economic activity, operating within the context of government control (i.e., a mixed economy). Through monetary (control of the money supply) and fiscal (taxation, budgetary allocations and magnitudes) policies, the state became the insurer of the public against market fluctuations severe enough to threaten society itself. The experience of the Depression and World War II demonstrated the power of public agencies to limit, alter, and redirect the marketplace for several different purposes. The primary purpose of permanent intervention was to prevent the socioeconomic conditions of the 1930s from occurring again.

Intervention for system maintenance is obviously related to redistributive policies in the Roosevelt years. The reformers and the Progressives had for a generation and more criticized the unrestrained marketplace, not only for its inherent instability but also for its failure to distribute wealth more evenly throughout society. Roosevelt discovered this insight to have particular utility in the polling booth during the 1930s. Millions of Hoover Republicans became "Roosevelt socialists" in the Depression.

In an important sense, the interventions of the Roosevelt years were essentially conservative approaches toward a welfare state. Nearly every program was directed toward helping people to become economically productive, if at all possible. Intervention during this period was mainly oriented toward private sector expansion. Intervention for system maintenance and the Alger myth were blended to make a rather neat, if contradictory, received value mix. The 1946 mix was discoverable in the institutions, laws, beliefs, and desires of the realm and is worth recapitulating.

The state stimulates and supports private enterprise, as it did in the first fifty years of the Republic. The bedrock of the economy rests on the initiative of the entrepreneur operating in an environment of minimal restraint through state regulation for expansion. The state intervenes in the market when and if signs of economic instability or external threat make it necessary. People unable to participate in the economy because of a lack of resources are to be assisted by the state to full participation in the private sector. Those unable to participate because of age or infirmity are to have the minima of existence guaranteed them by the state.

The implications and ramifications of this received value mix are still being felt. As radical and new as the permanent interventions of the Roosevelt years seemed, they pale in the face of the elaborations and additions to the received value mix that characterize the present era, whose genesis I mark with the passage of the Employment Act of 1946.

The Modern Era: Management of Complex Interdependence

The discovery by the national government that most of its acts had both direct and indirect effects on the economy was made in the Roosevelt period. The centralization of economic power in the public and private sectors proceeded apace after the war. The by-now institutionalized constituencies of big labor, big business, big agriculture, and big commerce were paralleled by big government. The shift noted above to the President as a prime actor in the realm of political economy during the Roosevelt era also involved a necessary devolution of authority from his office to the administrative arm of the state. This was *necessarily* so for a number of reasons.

(1) The sheer administrative task of operating the intervening agencies of a mixed economy was beyond the capability of any one office. The routinization of clerical tasks, alone, in the new areas of significance required a tremendous expansion of agency size. In addition, there was the propensity to create new agencies to deal with the new aspects of the realm of political economy. Old agencies like the Agriculture Department and the Treasury grew as elaborating subsystems of their domains became more significant. The Internal Revenue Service is an example of this. The states and the cities were "rediscovered," and their role in the national economy became more and more significant. As they became new points of intervention, their administrative agencies grew even more rapidly than those of the federal government. Other reasons for the bureaucratic expansion were at least as significant as the enormous growth of clerical, compliance, and housekeeping tasks.

(2) The traditional foci of lobbying, bargaining, and the representa-

tion of constituencies in the realm of political economy underwent a sharp change. The governments of the states, localities, and national government regulated and intervened through the creation of more and more administrative agencies and commissions operating under broad discretionary powers delegated by legislatures and executives. Housing authorities, public utility commissions, and regulatory agencies concerned with ever more specialized aspects of economic activity became most significant governmental actors. As the act of political definition included nearly every aspect of economic life, the classic means of constituency representation began to be discovered in bureaucratic agencies. Indeed, as it becomes evident that administrative and regulatory agencies are engaged in the allocation of scarce public resources, constituencies unsatisfied with the representational qualities of a particular agency may attempt to have legislation passed which creates an agency in competition. Today, the balancing of powerful interests brings about new administrative agencies. In the past it might have meant the temporary domination of legislatures and executives by one political party or the other. The process of agency proliferation can be discovered at all levels of government, then, in part as a function of the recognition by political actors that many vital aspects of economic intervention and regulation are in the hands of administrative agencies.

(3) As the economic activities of the private sector have grown as a result of an ever-refining division of labor, the task of comprehension for laymen has become ever more burdensome. American agriculture, industry, and commerce are so diversified and so highly technical that knowledge of special vocabularies and activities becomes essential to the tasks of intervention and regulation. Specialization of persons has followed specialization of task. The new actors defining the realms of political economy are likely to command highly specialized languages and skills.

The regulation and stimulation of atomic energy, for example, are conducted in the language of engineers and high finance. As this is being written, a public debate is being conducted about the safety hazards of nuclear plants. I define such a question as political. I note in passing that politicians not much better educated than I are supposed to decide the issue between the competing claims of engineers, industrial firms, and power companies. How is one to decide if one doesn't understand the language or methods of the opposing sets of engineers? Worse, how is one to know of the possibility of alternatives when the engineers are in complete agreement? The decisions of the engineers in this case are, I believe, the honest results of their applied expertise. Yet, what is done in regard to nuclear plant safety is quintessentially political. No electorate, no legislature, and no elected executive is prepared to ignore expertise. We live in an age in which our political choices are increasingly couched in technical languages with which we are unfamiliar. The state, then, must hire and depend upon its own experts in many areas of economic intervention and regulation.

The size and scope of regulation and intervention, the multifaceted nature of federalism and the economy itself, and the demands of expertise direct our attention to the realm of administrators, experts, commissions, and bureaucracies. The concomitant development of private sector expertise and public sector structures of expert regulation and intervention represents a continuation and elaboration of the Roosevelt years. An outstanding example of this general phenomenon began what I am calling the modern era and is worth a brief digression.

Since 1946 political struggles over macroeconomic policy have been thoroughly dominated by the vocabulary and analytical tools of university-trained economists. Liberal, conservative, and moderate *economists* are political actors of the first order, because they so thoroughly dominate the creation of decisional premises. Many distinguished economists of the modern era have served government in one capacity or another. Millions of Americans read the politico-economic prescriptions of Paul Samuelson and Milton Friedman in *Newsweek*. Presidents, congressmen, and judges are by necessity somewhat literate in the vocabulary and models of economics. Who, however, is competent to judge the likely effects of a change in the money supply, the rediscount rate, or the multiplier effect of some federal expenditure? Not this writer. Presidents, corporation executives, congressmen, and union leaders may engage in the debate by picking their economists. The definition of the problem, the statement of the decisional premises, and the predictions of the outcomes of a particular choice are no longer the exclusive turf of electoral politicians and private sector elites. This is not to claim that economists control macroeconomic policy or that Presidents do not make significant decisions. I am suggesting, however, that an academic discipline, unelected and "apolitical," has, through its ability to predict some kinds of events, come to dominate the political conception of the economy and thereby to exercise influence undreamed of even forty years ago.

The past twenty years has seen the revival of traditional roles within the received value mix of stimulation and support. The federal government reentered the infrastructure creation field (the construction of roads, canals, dams and communication systems necessary to the functioning of a modern economy) with vigor through organizational forms characteristic of the bureaucratic age. The Tennessee Valley Authority of the 1930s built dams and provided hydroelectric power for a disadvantaged region. Instead of direct government support for private entrepreneurs, the New Dealers created a structure of intervention and control that not only built dams and sold power but also developed elaborate constituent and clientele relationships among the populations of the several states it served.[9] Massive interventions using approximations of this model began to solidify in the states as well. The turnpike, bridge, port, and housing authorities became political realms in the states and were in some cases nearly outside the active control of the legislative and executive institutions that created them.[10] National, state, and local government interventions have altered the landscape more profoundly since 1946 than they had since the founding of the Republic.

Three policies serve to illustrate this claim and to identify the new structures of this realm. The Federal Highway Trust Fund was created during the Eisenhower years to provide for an interstate highway system, ostensibly for reasons of national defense. The fund was to be kept sound by taxation of the new lifeblood of commerce—gasoline. Proceeds were used to construct a highway system connecting cities throughout the nation. Access to urban centers was thereby enhanced considerably, and the travel time between places was reduced. Expressways, parkways, and thousands of miles of subsidiary roads were constructed. At the same time the federal government created a system (the FHA) which guaranteed mortgage monies loaned to home buyers by banks. The favored buyer was the buyer of a new house, because the long-term value of a new house was more certain than that of an older one. The most efficient, economical, and now easily accessible place to build that new housing lay

---

[9] In his classic *TVA and the Grass Roots* (New York: Harper, 1966), Philip Selznick approximates my notion of bureaucratic constituency in the process which he calls "informal co-optation," which "represents a mechanism of comprehensive adjustment, permitting a formal organization to enhance its chances for survival by accommodating itself to existing centers of interest and power within its area of operation" (p. 217). Formal co-optation resembles some aspects of bureaucratic clientele: "These new methods [of control] center around attempts to organize the mass, to change an undifferentiated and unreliable citizenry into a structured, readily accessible public" (p. 219).

[10] An outstanding example of this phenomenon is to be found in Robert A. Caro, *The Power Broker* (New York: Vintage, 1975).

in the areas surrounding the cities. Highway construction permitted one a short journey to work in the city, and FHA and VA loan guarantees created the possibility of buying relatively inexpensive new housing. In the memory of the relatively young, the nation was suburbanized. Federal and state policies accelerated and facilitated the move to the suburbs as surely as they had the expansion of the west three generations before.

At the same time that the move to the suburbs was being stimulated and supported, the renewal of the urban core was being attempted by agencies at all three levels of government. Urban renewal and housing programs were created in the late 1940s. Billions were spent in the decades that followed. The effect of these programs was to create thousands of jobs in the construction industry and to rebuild areas of the central business district in many cities. Most of the urban renewal expenditures resulted in nonresidential construction, and the prime beneficiaries of the program seemed to be the unions, banks, developers, speculators, and firms locating in the new facilities.

The highway, FHA, and urban renewal programs constituted a new form of middle-class welfare in that the beneficiaries of these programs were car and truck owners, young and middle-aged suburban homeowners (or would-be homeowners), and those for whom the central business district of cities was a place of employment, commerce, or amenity.[11] The promise of the Roosevelt years seemed to have been expanded to the point where a "new socialism" of a peculiarly American sort characterized much of the realm of political economy. This new socialism encompassed programs that ranged from farm price supports and oil depletion allowances to school lunch programs and Aid to Families with Dependent Children. Chapter four has much more to say about social welfare programs. At this point it is important to note that the expenditures by all levels of government rose enormously in the social welfare areas, particularly in public education.

With each expansion of government into new areas of stimulation and support came agencies of control and regulation. The agencies created since 1946 and their rising portions of the allocative pie tell part of the story. The Department of Health, Education and Welfare, the Department of Housing and Urban Development, and the Department of

[11] See Edward C. Banfield, *The Unheavenly City Revisited* (Boston: Little, Brown, 1974) for a similar view of this phenomenon.

Transportation are children of the modern era.[12] They and their counter-parts in the states and cities constitute emerging structures of power within the realm of political economy. Hybrid creations of state legisla-tures, interstate compacts, and federal bureaucratic initiative have de-veloped into highly significant political realms. The public authority, made up of public and private actors and governing some aspect of economic life independent of strict supervision from any element of tradi-tional political control, has become a fixture in many states and localities.

The politics of urban renewal, housing, highways, and development in general have become the politics of administrative agencies embodying legislative and representational systems heretofore discoverable only in traditional institutions. The New York Port Authority looks more like a Renaissance city-state than it does an instrument of American govern-ment. Not only is it a creation of two states responsible for operating port facilities in and around New York Harbor, but it also builds bus terminals and gigantic office buildings (the World Trade Center) and operates one of the largest police forces in the United States. The com-plexity and power of special-purpose districts, authorities, commissions, and bureaus make the task of description and analysis much more difficult than it ever was.

To further complicate the realm of political economy, I must mention briefly yet another child of 1946, which is the subject of chapter five. The Department of Defense was created in the Truman years to consolidate the demobilizing and presumably contracting war machine. For only a brief period did this new administrative creation go into the decline that had been traditional for armed forces after a war. The new war was a cold war, and the past two decades have seen an unprecedented involve-ment of the Defense Department in the realm of political economy. The technological imperative that had so thoroughly captured the minds of businessmen and consumers was nowhere more potent than in the De-fense Department. Huge investments in maintaining strategic superiority over our potential enemies were nearly matched by investments in devel-oping weapon systems of the future.

The politics of defense spending became a fixture in the realm of political economy. Large industrial firms entered into close and lasting relationships with the DOD. Vast sums were paid to relatively few cor-

---

[12] The Department of Health, Education and Welfare was created in 1953, Housing and Urban Development in 1965, and Transportation in 1966.

porations on a contractual basis which defied the market mechanism and
which constituted an extraordinary concentration of wealth and power.
The politics of this military–industrial complex caused President Eisenhower to be concerned for the future of democratic government in America.

We live in an era of discontinuous resource allocation, a function of
the competition between powerful actors organized into complex structures of control and interest aggregation. The realm of political economy
is the realm of powerful agencies of the state and their constituency
networks. It is the new constituency politics of formal organizations
rather than of legislatures to which I refer.

For every organized economic interest there is an agency at some
level of government. For every agency there is a constituency network
interdependent with it. Allocative decisions above the agency level are
competed for by the complex organizational structures of government
and their constituents. From the local elites who dominate the agricultural policies of their region through representation in the Agriculture
Department to the handful of aircraft manufacturers whose lifeblood is
defense contracts, the politics of the realm is highly organized and structured. In many ways this appears to be simply an expansion of the
private power argument of McConnell and the "interest group liberalism" phenomenon identified by Lowi.[13] It is in some ways. In other
important ways it is not.

Government power in the realm of political economy does not simply
consist of passive accommodation to the most powerful economic interests in society. Along about the time that Robert McNamara became
Secretary of Defense, it began to appear that government bureaucrats,
long insulated from the direct interference of politicians in most cases,
had interests of their own in deciding what should, could, and perhaps
would be policy. This came about in part when specialization of task and
devotion to technological change became cultural dogma. The problems
of complex interaction also began to become political questions that
tended to elevate the specialized bureaucrat to something greater than a
high-priced clerk. Entrepreneurial bureaucrats building empires of control are not a new story. What has developed in the modern era is a class
of bureaucrats who became the cutting edge of innovation and change in

---

[13] Grant McConnell, *Private Power and American Democracy* (New York: Knopf,
1967) and Theodore J. Lowi, *The End of Liberalism* (New York: Norton, 1969).

the realm of political economy in partnership with the private sector. Government itself became a prime generator of change through the combined efforts of bureaucrats and their constituents.

Defense contractors lay down not only with generals, admirals, and senators. The king-sized bed of the Defense Department was also roomy enough for systems analysts, comptrollers, and project directors. Patterns of domination, subordination, and partnership have developed between bureaucrats and constituents in a variety of settings involving not only high technology programs, but also programs that attempt to manage newly discovered aspects of complex economic and social interaction.[14]

The discovery and institutionalization of the business cycle as a system requiring government intervention and regulation was the key development of the Roosevelt years which I associate with the growing power of bureaucratic actors in the period 1933–1946. Since 1946 the agencies of intervention and participation in the realm of political economy have begun to notice complex interaction. By complex interaction I mean to describe the primary, secondary, and tertiary effects of government intervention. Every action of the state generates changes in the economic environment which interact with the effects of other actions of the state. Thus, agency X constructs a low-income, high-rise apartment complex; the effect of the structure on the new tenants seems ambiguous at best, since they proceed to destroy the buildings shortly after moving in. The banks, contractors, and union people who built the thing couldn't care less. The local police, school system, health department, and welfare system, to name but a few, do have a few financial problems as a result of the project. Who manages? Who is reponsible? The DOD closes a Navy shipyard and thereby immediately increases unemployment, which causes yet another drain on state and local agencies. Daily, one can find examples of complex interaction simply by reading the newspaper.

The past three decades have been the years of conglomerates, multinationals, and the expansion of consumer credit. Diversified international corporations with multiple identities inside and outside government jurisdiction make the job of regulation and intervention that much more complex. The expansion of consumer credit has permitted an unrivaled pattern of consumption dispersed throughout classes of wage earners,

[14] An outstanding book in this area is still Charles J. Hitch and Roland M. McKean, *The Economics of Defense in the Nuclear Age* (Cambridge: Harvard University Press, 1963).

who a generation ago would have been on the outside looking in at the world of two cars, the split-level, and the color TV.

The trusts are gone. They have been replaced by even larger monopolistic and oligopolistic entities thoroughly interdependent with government. One finds it difficult to draw any but sterile and legalistic distinctions between the government and, say, the telephone company. The marketplace has been suspended by the telephone company, and those who disapprove of their utility company had better check on its competition before having the lights turned off, because there isn't any competition. Several years ago that pulse of our cultural existence, the gross national product (GNP), crossed not only the magic trillion dollar mark but also told us that in the mix of goods and services, the latter accounted for more of the total than did the former.

Governments generate positive and negative externalities that have long-run and short-run consequences for the kinds of actions both public and private actors may take in the future. I doubt that a dozen people sat down and decided to create a suburbanized America in the 1950s. I do know that the net effect of a series of disconnected and disaggregated decisions was to stimulate and support a stupendous population movement. I do know that the educational and other services needed to support the new suburban population were inadequate, insufficient, or simply absent. We are now beginning to assess the effects of the program that stimulated this development. The list is nearly endless. More roads, more cars, and suddenly a shortage of gas that is terminal. More roads, more cars, and suddenly a multibillion dollar pollution bill. The present era is one which necessarily brings the matter of complex interdependence to the fore.

The national imperative to manage complex interdependence, interaction, and technological change is upon us. The managers of complex interdependence and those who structure the decisional premises of the actors who must choose among investments in technologies are not likely to be the familiar constituents of the realm of political economy alone. The unions, the banks, the corporations may limit and structure much of the environment of decision, as will members of Congress and judges. The drift, however, is toward expertise and specialization vested in the structure of government administrators and corporate technocrats.[15] The

---

[15] The term is, of course, from John Kenneth Galbraith, *The New Industrial State* (Boston: Houghton Mifflin, 1971). But I specifically reject his argument about the *primacy* of technocrats, even in high-technology organizations, public or private.

politics of pollution control, natural resource development, public welfare, and defense will involve changes in the realm of political economy.

The politics of this realm is historically founded on constituency relationships, and I believe that it will continue to be so based. The change from the past lies in the argument that the constituencies are and will increasingly become bureaucracy relevant rather than legislatively oriented. Managers, economists, planners, and all of those responsible for interfaces between complex systems are in the process of emerging as equals to the bankers, union chiefs, and corporate moguls of the past. The realm, if anything, will become more and more removed from the patterns of our daily existence as it becomes more and more determinative of them.

Constituency networks tend to dominate the realm of political economy and will continue to do so, because they concentrate their resources in pertinent issue clusters. Industries concerned with tariff problems, for instance, tend to gather together to influence congressmen, Commerce and State Department bureaucrats, and other public agencies dealing with foreign trade. Economic constituents are also heavily represented on the boards and commissions created to regulate them. I have suggested that the power of organized economic constituents is not uniformly determinative of policy outcomes. On the contrary, government itself is big business, and one must look with great care at each major policy or issue cluster in order to attempt to determine who is influencing whom for what purpose.

Often government functions as the referee between labor and management. Occasionally, it intervenes to regulate for the benefit of one "public" over another. The common case has been decision making out of the public eye. Incremental changes in tariffs, rates, the money supply, and the like are seldom matters of public attention during reasonably stable economic periods. Attention by political actors grows under crisis conditions only to evaporate under the blanket of mass media noise. The oil crisis of two years ago has disappeared from the public communications media. Public policy regarding the terminal nature of energy resources leading to the utter deterioration of industrialized society has been determined: The state has created a public bureaucracy (The Energy Research and Development Administration) to work on ways out of the dilemma. The oil companies are well diversified and ready for the coming crises. One knows what the state is up to and what the oil cartel is doing, but what of the individual constituent, client, and victim? Where do they fit into these issue-specific structures of economic control, regulation, and profitability?

Those individuals who hold stock in oil companies or own auto dealerships or belong to the Teamsters' Union may or may not have their interests represented at any given moment. They are constituents who can measure their benefits more easily than they can measure the degree to which their desires are being represented. When stock prices go down, when cars aren't selling, and when goods shipped over the roads decrease, what are these individuals? They may be *clients* able to adjust temporarily. They are unlikely to band together to alter the actions of the elites who dominate the constituent organizations to which they belong or upon whom they depend.

What of the nonunionized employee, the salaried white-collar worker, the domestic, and the small businessman? Unemployment turns these kinds of people into *clients* of the state, dependent upon the largesse of government to assist them as they eat into the cheapening dollars of inflation ravaged savings. In good times they are either directly or indirectly dependent upon the positive effects of constituent organizations, because they are part of their networks. The white-collar worker in a medium-sized industrial corporation exists in an organizational setting that is highly dependent upon the actions of more powerful aggregations of economic power. Suppliers of capital, raw materials, and wholesale markets interdependent with government agencies control the fate of his organization and ultimately of his job. He has few alternatives in hard times. The same chain, slightly varied, is discoverable for the nonunion employee (and for those in relatively weak unions), the domestic, and the small businessman.

Victims are all too easy to identify. The unemployed who possess outmoded skills and who cannot afford retraining or are too old for it are victims. The children of those who earn marginal wages are victims when inflation reduces their diets to subsistence levels and below. The retired who live on fixed incomes are ruined by inflation and real estate tax increases. Most victims never comprehend the sets of macroeconomic forces that make their lives miserable. Nor do I know all these forces or understand the ones that I do know.

I do recall one matter, however. All the people discussed above are *citizens* of the United States. As such, one may legitimately question the meaning of that exalted term as it applies in the realm of political economy. In point of fact, the term "citizen" seems absurd in this context.

We are a nation of consumers who pursue material comfort and convenience to excess. This sentiment is common enough. What is curious is the distinction between citizenship and consumership. One suspects that in the realm of political economy the former is subsumed by the latter.

Yet, it is also true that some of us consume more than others. Some of us can control what, how, and when we consume, and some of us cannot. Most of us are beneficiaries of the realm of political economy, but very few of us are represented in the political processes that enhance benefit.

The general and systemic costs of American capitalism are only now becoming apparent to large numbers of consumers. The frictions that arise from the unequal distribution of wealth and the ability to consume remain serious political concerns removed from the day-to-day actions of most individuals. The unanticipated and consequential costs of water and air pollution as well as the depletion or destruction of natural resources have "suddenly" been added to the familiar problems of capitalism. Despite the fact that increasing numbers of us notice the "new" problems, one looks in vain for a general representational mode that can be used to mobilize the state to act in majoritarian interests.

The Realm of Political Economy: A Received Value Mix

The laws, rules, customs, beliefs, and desires that have regulated and directed agencies of the state and their constituencies over time in the realm of political economy are far more complex than the six general values that I believe characterize the received value mix.

Those entities of a received value mix which are most readily identifiable are, of course, formal structures of action in the form of agencies and organizations of one sort or another. The realm of political economy today contains literally thousands of public and private organizations more or less dedicated to their self-interest under one or more of the six major received values outlined above. Patterns of conflict and cooperation over the allocation of scarce public resources are discoverable throughout organized social existence. The role of the state and the distinction between that which is public and that which is private have in the past two centuries changed almost beyond recognition. Yet, I think that the elements of the received value mix of this realm have shown significant resiliency through time.

The values of *stimulation* and *support* for the private sector through an increasing number of direct and indirect actions of the state are even more significant today than they were during the era of Hamilton's *Report on Manufactures* or Clay's American System. Constant redefinitions of the political and of the role of the state have made government agencies permanent actors in repeating cycles of stimulation and support through a variety of methods and structures.

The persistence of *laissez faire individualism* in the form of legislation and institutions that intervene to support this value is one of those enduring contradictions that accounts for persistent interrealm conflict. The doctrine and my use of the term certainly are transformed from the nineteenth century, although Ayn Rand buffs probably still carry the torch of purity (largely of their own making). One of the great inventions of the last century was the marvelous fiction that made the corporation into something like an individual but limited its liability unlike an individual. If we are allowed to engage in this legalistic reification of organizations (pretending that corporations are in some ways like persons) and if the reader will permit the outrageous transmogrification, then one can see that the modern industrial corporation is that "rugged individual" who has certain rights. The spirit and forms of laissez faire individualism inhere in many organizations large and small, and this value partially accounts for the fact that one speaks of a mixed economy rather than a planned economy.

Much of the meaning of laissez faire can be accounted for by the representations of large private corporations struggling to resist government interference which they believe not beneficial to their interests. One should not conclude that this value represents the very worst of capitalist ideology. Laissez faire individualism does include the corporate right to foul our air, but it also contains the seeds of a system of planning, growth, and risk that has benefited more people more thoroughly than any other system in history. Like each value in the mix, this one is a mixed blessing.

Regulation for expansion represents an attempt to balance interests in almost classic Madisonian form.[16] The rights of the manufacturer to

---

16 Madison, in *The Federalist Papers* and later Tocqueville in *Democracy in America* recognized the private association, economic interest, religious group and region as being factors which served the cause of developing a nation state. Para-

exploit land, labor, and capital for his benefit and for the benefit of his stockholders have to be balanced against the public interest. The public interest seems to lie not only in reasonably unrestrained trade opportunities (following the laissez faire argument) but also in seeing that its welfare is protected in a number of other areas. Thus, no one may sell adulterated meat or dangerous drugs, despite the fact that impairment of that ability constitutes an intervention into unfettered capitalism. This sentiment seems banal to us today simply because it is a part of the received value mix. The logic of such intervention has carried us far beyond a Pure Food and Drug Law and into a host of conflicting and complex regulatory values that may or may not be directed toward expansion. In general, however, only the most noxious and flagrantly undesirable practices have been diminished, and I believe that the general posture of regulatory agencies has been toward expansion of that which is regulated.

The great disasters of the 1930s and 1940s altered the received value mix in such a way that *intervention for system maintenance* has become a fixture of political structure. The problems of system maintenance include not only violent fluctuations in the business cycle but also the problems of defense, pollution, and resource depletion. Permanent intervention through the structures of economic control and through the maintenance of a powerful peacetime military establishment is thoroughly embedded in the realm of political economy. The scope of the latter is grand enough to be included in discussion of more than one realm. The same is true for the welfare state. The distributive and redistributive policies of the Roosevelt era have been expanded to include economic and social "rights" beyond even the fertile imagination of Harry Hopkins. I will attempt to deal with this overlapping realm in the next chapter. At this point it is sufficient to note that the state went into the insurance business in a big way during the period 1933–1946, and it has been expanding its trade ever since. By "insurance" I mean to suggest that the nation is now (imperfectly, to be sure) insured against depression and against outside attack. Individuals are now insured (again imperfectly)

---

doxically, such divisions were simultaneously perceived as being potential sources of disunity. Madison and his latter-day interpreters and elaborators attempted to reconcile this paradox by formulating a notion of the state as "referee" between conflicting factions and interests, thus establishing the state as an essentially neutral element charged with enforcing the "rules of the game." Modern reformulations can be discovered in the work of Bentley, Truman and Dahl.

against want from lack of food, fiber, and shelter. The expansion of the matters covered by such "insurance" has increased tremendously, and the idea of permanent intervention for system maintenance is embedded in a host of institutions, laws, and structures.

The final value identified is *management of complex interdependence,* a term I believe characterizes much of the value contribution of the modern era. I suppose that it is best to say explicitly that complex interdependence is in fact *not* being managed. Rather, I believe the modern era to be a period when such management is deemed desirable and when powerful actors are indeed attempting to manage. They are far from successful, however, for many reasons, most of which stem precisely from the contradictory nature of the realm's received value mix. To further complicate matters, the state of knowledge regarding the operation of that which we hopefully and presumptuously call "the system" is, to be charitable, incomplete. We are just now developing an academic discipline called "policy analysis," which is an attempt in part to discover the interactive effects and ramifications of any given intervention.

Among the more successful managers of complex interdependencies in the modern era have been the large industrial and service corporations. They have managed to plan years in advance of changes in the market. They predict levels of consumer demand, materials for supply, capitalization needs, and probable labor costs well in advance of the introduction of any new product or service. Their capacity to predict is, of course, not insignificantly related to their ability to manipulate markets through advertising and to control variability in the supply of materials, labor, and capital. This management of risk and uncertainty in situations of complex interdependence is no small achievement.

The commodity that makes the management of risk and uncertainty possible under conditions of complex interdependence is highly evolved expertise. The possession of analytical tools is no assurance of moral superiority or right reason. Indeed, the mere existence of specialized persons and groups who possess both knowledge and the power to allocate scarce public resources is no guarantee of "good" decisions. My claim is that the realm of political economy in the last quarter of the twentieth century has come to be dominated by public bureaucracies and their constituency networks. Political economy is characterized almost entirely by constituency relationships that involve varying equilibria of power between complex organizations, some of which are clothed in the mantle of the state and some of which are not.

The received value mix, then, contains the complementary and contradictory elements I have discussed. It has displaced the simpler political realms of legislatures and courts for presidents and bureaucrats over the past two hundred years of conflict and cooperation. As policy alters through one or all of the means and reasons discussed in chapter two, the realm of the political will change, and the ephemeral policy of yesterday will become the fixed aspect of structure today. There is much about the realm of political economy to suggest that a set of relatively new actors representing a mix of relatively modern and antique values will be discovered in large formal organizations.

chapter four

The Realm
of Social Welfare
and Control

Introduction: From Sewerage to Moral Philosophy

The old-fashioned legal term for the social welfare and control policies of the state is "the police power." This was ordinarily construed to cover matters of public health, safety, and welfare (or morals). In keeping with this definition, the pages that follow include discussion and analysis of matters as diverse as social security, crime, and public education. Many substantive issues, programs, and policies are not considered. Some overlap with the realms of political economy and national defense, and some do not. The central point of the chapter is to illustrate the differing forms certain key conceptual elements take when one moves from matters of political economy to the substance of social welfare and control.

At those vague points where the state meets its environment through public bureaucracies, the realm of social welfare and control is most profoundly one of clients and victims. The idea of clientele is rather sharply bifurcated in this realm. The bulk of social security recipients is a clientele in much the same way that most of us are clients of large economic organizations. There is, of course, at least one essential difference. Social security beneficiaries are directly dependent upon the state. In general, they are passive recipients who, while they number in the millions, are not particularly active politically *as social security benefi-*

ciaries. Their presence may be significant to legislators who may fear that reductions in benefits will lead to their mobilization *as electoral constituents.* But as a general proposition, social security beneficiaries, like the rest of us, seldom interact for any prolonged period with political bureaucracy.

A second client population consists of those who are directly confronted by public bureaucrats in significant face-to-face interactions. The poor, the impoverished sick, the unemployed, the public school student, the mental patient, the apprehended criminal, and all of those citizens whose day-to-day lives depend upon and are partially defined by agents of the state make up this second population.

The constituent/client/victim taxonomy is also examined *within the state,* in order to illustrate how different received values and realm structures lead to politics that differ significantly from that of political economy and national defense. Since the environment of the realm contains few constituencies, public bureaucratic claimants are the significant actors. There is nothing in the realm of social welfare and control to compare to the AFL-CIO or the oil oligarchy. Rather, the public bureaucracies work to *represent themselves and their clients and victims as if they were constituents.*

Within the realm received values are held with varying degrees of passion by legislative and bureaucratic actors. Some bureaucratic actors have, over time, managed to have their values and programs enshrined in the traditional allocative patterns of legislatures. The FBI is an example of this. Other actors who claim to represent clients and victims are less successful. Public welfare expenditures and the ups and downs in federal aid to education illustrate in part the failure of the appropriate bureaucratic actors to become allocative fixtures like the FBI.

Despite these differences within the environment of the realm and within the realm itself, public expenditures on social welfare and control have become the dominant feature of budget documents at most levels of government in the past generation. There are few indications that this situation will change drastically in the near future, although one might reasonably predict some leveling off to occur in areas such as public higher education. There are ominous signs that some expenditures may have "uncontrollable" aspects that could lead to serious interrealm conflict. This is particularly so in the case of national defense and social welfare spending.

The matter of professionalization in the social welfare and control bureaucracies is considered throughout the following analysis because it is central to the two matters mentioned above: Professionalized bureaucrats define client and victim relationships and act as constituents within the realm of social welfare and control.

Institutionalization, Moral Superiority, and Philanthropy: 1789–1933

From the beginning of the Republic to the present there have been two sets of social welfare policies and populations. The first and most numerous involved the ordinary functions of government. Those functions concerned with the common needs of the citizenry included matters of health, sanitation, public safety, and education. The cities and towns of colonial America created such public facilities and services for general use. The education of the young, while limited and largely private in the eighteenth century, was nevertheless generally considered to be a matter of public concern, as was the protection of life and limb through primitive police forces, fire brigades, and other protective organizations. Libraries and other amenities were founded in cities and in some towns. These were often created by philanthropy, private organizations, and public agencies or some combination thereof. One starts, then, with the idea of ordinary consumers of public goods. All citizens were entitled to such benefits because they paid taxes or use fees. Those unable to pay could in many instances partake, since some public goods such as libraries and parks are in effect indivisible. (There is no practical way to allocate benefits according to contribution.)

The second set of policies and populations differed from the first in that they were (and are) characterized by the problems of personal stigma. Those defined as criminals, mental incompetents, paupers, orphans, and the like were precluded from full participation as citizens because of their dependence upon the state. This dependence arose in part as a function of the definition of one's malady or deprivation. It also arose from economic and social class differences. Those unable to be maintained by their families were (and are) most likely to be those of modest means. Obviously, the stigma of poverty in most eras pertains to one socioeconomic class. One speaks not of rich orphans when one talks about juvenile centers or orphanages. Insanity of the rich and the near-rich was a matter of private concern, even when it involved institutionalization. Private sanitoria and clinics have always made the insanity of the well-to-do a private matter, while the mental illness of the common folk was a matter of public policy. The same was (and to some extent is) true of physical illness. For most of the period 1789–1933 similar distinctions pertained to post-secondary education as well, although this can be overstated. Public policy as regards this second population was directed at persons who were defined by stigma and by socioeconomic class. This was true in the nineteenth century and is far from absent in our own time. To define stigma as a concern of the state and then to categorize people accordingly is most profoundly an act of political definition.

The two populations correspond roughly to my distinctions between constituents, clients, and victims. Those who paid taxes and were ordinary residents of the county or town were constituents of the school boards, libraries, and whatnot created by them for their welfare and that of the citizenry in general.

The second population was essentially a set of clients and victims which in the last century might have been divided into "deviants" and "unfortunates." "Unfortunates" were those who by virtue of conditions over which they had no control came to be dependent upon others. Orphans without kin, the mentally ill and retarded, and those unable to work or who could not find employment were considered to be "unfortunate," while those who committed crimes or who chose not to work were "deviants." This distinction was not as clear in practice as might be inferred by my definition, however. In part this was because of the nature of the institutions created to solve the different kinds of social problems. Total institutions, created in hopes of redemption, rapidly deteriorated into places of harsh discipline, social isolation, and punishment. The penitentiary, the asylum, and the poorhouse of the nineteenth century were very similar institutions.[1] Separation from society for purposes of restoration and reformation created or enhanced social stigma by virtue of having removed people from their natural environments for long periods of time.

---

[1] This point is illustrated throughout David J. Rothman, *The Discovery of the Asylum* (Boston: Little, Brown, 1971). Much of my discussion of nineteenth-century thought on institutionalization comes from this outstanding book. A most penetrating work on such institutions in the contemporary period is Erving Goffman's *Asylums* (New York: Anchor, 1961). Rothman does not cite Goffman in his analysis of nineteenth-century institutions, yet the similarity of their descriptions, separated by discipline and historical period, is riveting.

In general, politics and policies in the realm of social welfare during this period were decentralized and discontinuous. Pleas for social change emanated from a variety of sources, but few public resources were actually allocated to assist the populations in need. The political machines, private agencies, and churches were the prime political realms. Compared with what was to come, they were relatively ineffectual.

Three values discoverable in this period have endured in the laws, structures, beliefs, and desires that bound the realm of social welfare. *Institutionalization* is discoverable throughout the contemporary realm. There are still many professional social service people and politicians who believe that removal from society is the first, crucial step on the therapeutic road to successful adaptation to society. Drug addicts, alcoholics, psychotics, and all kinds of criminals are sequestered for varying lengths of time in state institutions so that employees of the government (physicians, social workers, penologists, etc.) can have the opportunity to work their therapeutic wonders.

Philanthropy is still an important value in the social welfare mix. Federal income tax laws permit charitable deductions, thus stimulating the growth of private donations. This source of funds is important in a number of areas, especially private higher education, hospitals, and cultural centers. The great fortunes of many of the moguls of the late nineteenth and early twentieth centuries have been at least partially diverted by their owners or heirs to private foundations whose purposes are charitable or cultural and whose incomes are not taxed. Most private philanthropy does not come from these giants, however. Small givers to the United Fund, the Red Cross, and to thousands of church-centered social welfare activities are found throughout the social order. Private charitable hospitals and disease-specific charities abound. There is a cooperative range and variety of services provided to the public by private agencies that probably would not otherwise be available. Furthermore, there may be useful tensions between the uniformities of public social welfare structures and those which are supported by private philanthropy, particularly in the area of higher education.

We have also received a presumption of *moral superiority* in the provision of social services which is easily located in nineteenth-century thought. The recipients of social services are not believed to be capable of making their own decisions about the nature of the services they receive. The structures of social welfare reflect this today despite the so-called revolution in participation of the 1960s. The state repeatedly delegates the power to decide what is best to the professionals and administrators who dominate the realm. Laws and regulations of social welfare are formulated and applied in the recipient's interest without consulting him, as though his right to decide in matters of education or therapy were somehow less significant than his right to vote in, say, presidential primaries. As we shall see, the moral superiority of the last century is now clothed in the mantle of professionalism and expertise, often disguising the old "I know what is best for you" with robes, degrees, and jargon. People who exercise such power and who are representatives of the state are engaged in a political act obfuscated by widespread acceptance of profession as a detached, disinterested, and independent source of knowledge and therefore, power.

Professionalization and Federalization: 1933–1954

As in the realm of political economy, the New Deal social welfare response to the Great Depression brought great changes in politics and policy. In the social welfare realm the transformation to an increasingly centralized, federal configuration of power was, if anything, even more dramatic. Unemployment compensation, direct relief, construction programs, and the like were managed by administrative agencies created out of whole cloth or by traditional departments like the Department of the Interior. The states and cities were either bypassed or made to follow federal guidelines. By the late 1930s the Supreme Court had begun the long process of legitimating and then extending the federal presence in the social welfare realm. In 1954 it thrust the federal government into the complex area of racial integration of the public schools. The Supreme Court and the federal courts in general asserted that the national government had duties and responsibilities in a variety of areas in the social welfare and control realm which had previously been within the purview of the states.

Through the growing dominance of federal administration, progressive and liberal ideals guided action in the areas of poverty, unemployment, housing, health, and education. In the 1930s the poverty stigma of the "second," client, population had suddenly and dramatically shifted to the "first," constituent, group, so that the moral superiority of the ordinary taxpayer suffered a dent of sufficient severity to permit wide-scale acceptance of temporary federal relief and long-term federal insurance. The nation became locked into a Social Security system which guaranteed to all minimal retirement payments as well as support in periods of temporary unemployment. Enforced Social Security payments for middle income families were and are, of course, highly regressive taxes, but the idea that such a system is a proper and "liberal" function of the federal government was one of the important acts of political definition of the period. Widespread acceptance of the idea was highly significant to the growth of administrative power within the realm. The federal power to dominate the realm of social welfare and control through administrative agencies was firmly established during the period 1933–1954.[2]

The states were perceived by the new bureaucrats in Washington as administratively and ideologically inappropriate foci for the development of a welfare state. Centralization of resources seemed a good idea, given the ineffectiveness of the states in dealing with the crises of the early 1930s. The states were also viewed by the New Dealers as bastions of conservatism, corruption, and inequity. The federal Civil Service was believed to be a potential source of enlightened disinterest, aloof and above the clubhouse and courthouse politics of the cities and states. This persistent belief underpinned many of the New Deal ventures into the social welfare realm. Social problems became national problems with bureaucratic foci as powerful actors cooperated and conflicted within the realm and at its margins.

The accretion of "problem" areas was rapid and extensive. At first there were the matters of poverty and unemployment discussed in chapter three. The alphabet soup agencies developed their own regional organizations independent of the states. Where state entities were involved in administration through block grants or other mechanisms, strict federal guidelines were laid down and enforced by a growing army of federal employees. The federal presence grew rapidly into the areas of agriculture, housing, welfare, and eventually into education, crime, and a variety of health programs. This expansion involved interrealm conflict at state and national levels as well as intrarealm competition between and among bureaucratic and legislative actors. In general, the highly organized bureaucrats won, and they did so by taking a leaf from the oldest of political books.

Federal bureaucrats assumed the high ground by identifying prob-

[2] The literature on this period is extensive. I have found *The Secret Diary of Harold L. Ickes* (New York: Simon & Schuster, 1953) particularly insightful. Ickes was one of the premier social welfare bureaucrats and his unsparingly blunt descriptions of interrealm conflict and cooperation are very helpful to an understanding of the realm and its politics.

lems as national, nonpolitical, and capable of professional (and therefore disinterested) solution. To this claim they added the familiar behaviors of log-rolling and pork barrel, thus insuring that legislators, unhappy, uncertain, or contrary, could publicly identify federal contributions to their constituents' welfare as being in part their doing. Those who failed to understand the new players in the old game were "purged." Roosevelt and those who learned at his knee understood that the "new politics" in America was rooted in social welfare and political economy patronage administered by federal agencies. The day of the courthouse and clubhouse was passing, although certain significant social matters that provided bedrock for some politicians were left relatively untouched. One in particular is of crucial importance to an understanding of subsequent change: The federal government remained blind to racial discrimination.

Segregation, racial conflict, and all manner of discrimination against blacks remained the "hidden issue" in American politics during this period, and no administrative action of any significance took place during the era.[3] The Ku Klux Klan reared its hooded head forthrightly and publicly during the 1920s and 1930s. It appeared throughout the South and in many midwestern states. Lynching was all too common. The strict segregation of public facilities and neighborhoods, factories, and enterprises of all sorts was ignored. It was not until hundreds of thousands of blacks had served in the armed forces in two world wars that the federal government got around to desegregating the military. This occurred under the Truman administration, and it took another twenty years before the order began to be enforced in any serious way.

The failure of the New Dealers to deal with the rank injustice to blacks can be accounted for in a variety of ways. Essentially, fear of white reaction and the political clout of long-entrenched southern congressmen and senators pushed the issue far down on the agenda, if indeed it was ever on it to begin with. The treatment of blacks was considered a problem peculiar to the South, despite bloody race riots in Chicago in 1919 and in Detroit in 1943. Blacks were invisible to those who could see social injustice everywhere else. They were beyond discussion to the millions who believed them to be in their rightful place. It was the great "nonissue" of the period.

---

[3] The classic statement on this point is Ralph J. Bunche, *The Political Status of the Negro in the Age of FDR*, Dewey Grantham, ed. (Chicago: University of Chicago Press, 1973). Bunche makes a case for black participation in the AAA cotton elections as the first significant black electoral participation in the South.

Administrative power at the federal level was growing in other areas that logically might have had great effect upon the lot of blacks. This period saw the emergence of a full-scale federal police power in the area of criminal justice. Yet it took a whole generation and a variety of laws before the basic question of black suffrage in federal elections became a matter for the criminal justice system at the national level. Three kinds of justifications underlay the development and expansion of federal power in the area of enforcement.

Administrative enforcement of laws and rules, said to emanate from the commerce clause of the Constitution, provided the basis for expanding the mission, personnel, and resources of the Federal Bureau of Investigation. Crudely put, anything "involved" in interstate commerce or any movement across state lines after commission of certain felonious acts fell within the responsibility of one federal police agency or another. Drugs, prostitution, conspiracy, bank robbery (after all, banks had become federally insured), kidnapping, hijacking, and any robbery involving goods moving in interstate commerce came under the jurisdiction of the FBI. The agency had the good fortune of being led by one of the most outstanding bureaucratic politicians of the modern age. J. Edgar Hoover's rise to utter domination of law enforcement in the United States provides a blueprint for at least one type of bureaucratic entrepreneur. From the relative obscurity of a corrupt and lazy minor agency arose a colossus of bureaucratic power.

Hoover and his minions took advantage of several environmental factors to aid in the expansion of the agency. The emergence of organized crime from the Prohibition period, the sensationalization of the gangster, the Lindberg kidnapping, and the threat of internal subversion from foreign enemies, real and imagined, became occasions for FBI growth, and the agency capitalized on them to the fullest. Hoover was the first great bureaucratic publicizer. No bureaucrat had ever invested as much time and effort in publicizing the heroic efforts of his agency.[4] No politician short of Roosevelt was as sensitive to and manipulative of the emerging possibilities of the mass media. Hoover capitalized on and embellished a posture of incorruptibility, professionalism, and indispensability that could be a model for the development of bureaucratic power. He created a national academy for his own agents and local police which was

---

[4] Robert Moses was a close second. See Robert A. Caro's *The Power Broker* (New York: Vintage, 1975).

the legitimizing professional educational agency for the law enforcement community. He imposed high standards of personal conduct on his agents and brought to bear the latest technologies for the detection of crime, never failing to publicize the fact.

National data collection, first through fingerprinting and then through computerized filing of arrest records, security checks, and group affiliations, became a hallmark of the agency. The Ten Most Wanted List became a fixture on the post office wall and later on the TV screen. Hoover developed a public persona that enabled him to deal with Congress, presidents, and nominal superiors in the Attorney General's office as if they were allies rather than superiors. No thought of reducing the budget of the FBI could be understood to be less than suspect. Cavil at requests for increased resources was met with similar suspicion.

The problems of national security in wartime and in the cold war period brought the FBI into direct competition with the security-related agencies that grew out of the Departments of State and War. President Truman created the Central Intelligence Agency out of the wartime Office of Strategic Services. Unlike the Bureau of Narcotics which was staffed mainly by ex-FBI agents, the CIA had its personnel roots in the State Department and military departments. The CIA–FBI conflicts over jurisdiction and resources were classic cases of interrealm conflict. The obvious conflict arose over the question of who was responsible for domestic activities (counterintelligence) and who was to do the foreign work (intelligence). Agency charters and executive agreements could never quite eliminate the interrealm conflict as each group sought to gain hegemony over the domain of the other. Each was backed by powerful actors in the general political system, and each sought to maximize its budgetary share. Both agencies grew enormously during the period, and both violated their legal charters. The revelations of the Watergate case highlighted some of the violations, bringing to public attention some notion of the scope and powerful independence of these agencies.[5]

The FBI is essentially a federal police force whose statutory au-

[5] Strictly speaking, of course, one should not discuss the CIA in the social welfare realm. Unfortunately, the CIA, the Department of the Army, and other foreign policy and defense agencies have had a nasty habit of domain expansion which not only upsets my typology but causes fear and loathing among many people in and out of politics. For ample documentation of such domain expansion see U.S., Congress, Senate, *Foreign and Military Intelligence* and *Intelligence Activities and the Rights of Americans,* Final Report of the Select Committee to Study Governmental Operations. April 26, 1976.

thority begins with the commerce clause of the Constitution.[6] The CIA derives its legal justification from the presidency as the sole source for the conduct of foreign relations. Both agencies and their associated agencies (i.e., the Drug Enforcement Administration and the FBI, the National Security Agency and the CIA) have had a tendency to encroach upon the other's domain. As they expanded their resources, they expanded their missions, and they did so with and without the consent of Congresses and presidents. The commerce clause agencies and the national security agencies developed powerful capacities for investigation, intelligence, and coercion. As substantial and significant as these realms became, the administrative sanctions built into a variety of federal laws became almost as formidable.

This third justification for federal power lies in the "simple" logic of administration. Failure to comply with the regulations of an agency may bring withdrawal of funds. This seems simple enough when one speaks of fraud or malfeasance. What this essentially "housekeeping" power was to become, however, was far more serious. State and local officials who fail to comply with federal standards and guidelines in one area may have funds held up or eliminated in another, seemingly unrelated, area. If, for example, a college receiving no direct federal aid should fail to have the appropriate quota of women in its administration, HEW may prevent its students from obtaining guaranteed federal loans or federal scholarship aid. The National Science Foundation may hold up or cancel research funds. In other words, the federal administrative power to "police" states, localities, private colleges, hospitals, and businesses through indirect sanctions constitutes a third source of federal power with potential per-

---

[6] With the introduction of the Criminal Justice Reform Act of 1975 (S.1) in the Senate, federal jurisdiction over law enforcement threatened to extend into areas previously under state and local jurisdiction. The bill covered everything from a definition of culpable states of mind to standards of procedure for the application of death sentences. Almost every crime would have become a federal crime under S.1. Arson, for example, is drawn into the domain of federal jurisdiction under conditions such as the following:

> . . . the property that is the subject of the offense is moving in interstate or foreign commerce, or constitutes or is a part of an interstate or foreign shipment; is used in an activity affecting interstate or foreign commerce; is owned by, or is under the care, custody, or control of an organization receiving financial assistance from the United States; (or when) the United States mail or a facility of interstate or foreign commerce is used in the planning, promotion, management, execution, or concealment of the offense, or in the distribution of the proceeds of the offense. . . .

See U.S., Congress, Senate, S.1., January 15, 1975, p. 132.

haps in excess of that of such agencies as the FBI and the CIA. All three powers grew in scope and intensity during this period. They accelerated in the modern era as the federal presence in all public matters and many private ones increased dramatically.

The crowning common justification for the wide variety of new federal health, welfare, and police powers lay not so much in particular legal or political argument, for these often have a tendency to disappear. Public zeal for New Deal expansion probably had dropped considerably by the time Dwight D. Eisenhower became president. Those powers did not disappear, and they were not significantly contracted during the Eisenhower years, in part because of the growing acceptance of professionalization as a legitimating force behind the exercise and acceptance of administrative power in the social welfare and control realm.

Professionalization[7] involves the adoption of standards of practice, personal conduct, and qualification through education and/or examination. Professions administer their own standards for each of these matters and constitute some of the most politically powerful forces in the realm of social welfare and control. The states certify and license dozens of professions by adopting the dominant exclusionary codes stated by the appropriate professional organization. The medical profession is a model for the phenomenon. Its dominant professional group, the American Medical Association, sets the standards for admission to practice in cooperation with the medical schools it recognizes. Most states simply accept this process. Presidents now routinely submit lists of Supreme Court candidates to the American Bar Association for its approval. Professionalization, thus, is an extraordinarily important legitimating force for the exercise of individual power, and it becomes even more potent when mobilized into formal aggregations of state power.

New professions rose to great heights of political power during the period under discussion. The study of social work and the legitimization of social workers were greatly stimulated by federalization in the public

---

[7] Discussion of professionalization can be found throughout the literature of public administration and organization theory. Some useful material and interesting arguments can be found in: Frederick Mosher, *Democracy and the Public Service* (New York: Oxford University Press, Inc., 1968); W. Lloyd Warner et al., *The American Federal Executive* (New Haven: Yale University Press, 1963); Victor Thompson, *Modern Organization* (New York: Knopf, 1964); Amitai Etzioni, *Modern Organizations* (Englewood Cliffs, N.J.: Prentice-Hall, 1964); and Robert Golembiewski and Michael Cohen, *People in Public Service: A Reader in Public Personnel Administration* (Itasca, Ill.: Peacock, 1970).

welfare realm. Universities developed special degrees, and public and private agencies eventually came to be dominated by such degree recipients, thus guaranteeing that passage into those agencies would be granted only to those with the proper credentials. The public education sector received similar treatment.

The complex elaboration of professions under the division of labor is a reasonably familiar story. Specialization of function devolves into ever-refined categories of knowledge, characterized by increasingly technical and abstruse vocabularies; hence, the familiar designations of specialist and expert—hand surgeons, maritime lawyers, psychiatric social workers, third-grade language arts curriculum specialists, and so on *ad nauseam*.

Professionalization is significant to the realms of the political in a number of ways. First, the definition of the "problem" will have much to do with the range of alternative solutions considered by politicians and administrators. Problems are likely to be conceived of within the context of the operating norms of the profession. To the degree to which politicians, administrators, and the public generally believe in the validity of the profession, the decisional premises of that profession are likely to predominate over any alternatives. Indeed, it is often the case that all of the decisional premises (including conflicting ones) emanate from the same professional actors. This becomes particularly significant when those actors are also structured into large public organizations with an oligopoly of resources. The ultimate fusion of profession and administration comes when the agency itself is the major legitimating source of the profession, as was the case with Hoover and his FBI academy.

A second source of power derives from the fact that legislation is seldom self-enforcing. That is, legislation is nearly always open to interpretation and is inevitably written to grant discretionary powers to those who administer it. Practice may vary from agency to agency and over-arching norms of practice involving personal conduct and the handling of funds limit the play of professional norms. But within these boundaries and those of hierarchy and personnel practice laid down by the civil service commissions of governments, laws get enforced through administrative rule making that is largely contingent upon professional norms, especially in the realm of social welfare.

Professionalization of any function has great organizational significance. To professionalize may mean to centralize standards of conduct while decentralizing organizational actors. Professionals need less direct supervision in general than nonprofessionals, but they do require support services such as laboratories, clerical assistance, and the like. One may, therefore, expect organizations to develop patterns of decentralized operation (depending upon task) with a concomitant centralization of such administrative functions as budgeting, accounting, personnel, and rule making.[8]

This realm differs from the political economy realm in part because of the domination of professionals, but more importantly because of the nature of the problems and people with whom it must deal. Criminals, delinquents, poor people, students, the physically and mentally ill, and retired persons are not the stuff of bureaucratic constituency politics. No matter how significant our friends the economists have become, the powerful constituents of the realm of political economy are at least as significant, because they possess vital resources. More importantly, the constituents of the realm of political economy can affect the electoral arena in a number of ways that are familiar to most students of American politics.

There may be people in government who have something to say about the cultural deprivation of bankers, but such people are not likely to be nearly as significant to their constituents as those in the social welfare realm are to their clients when they proclaim that black children suffer from cultural deprivation. Social welfare professionals structured into large public organizations diagnosed that disease in response to politicians' desires to "do something" about the education of black children; they "knew better" than the potential recipients of the service. Woe betide the Treasury official, however, who simply "knows better" than American bankers and seeks to start a program or to promulgate rules without fully consulting their leadership. It matters little if the fellow does know better in some objective sense. One of the things about which such an official should know is that the fellows down at the Bank of America, Chase Manhattan, and the First National City Bank of New York had better be consulted if he wishes to exercise any discretion in the future. That is, if he has a future.

This illustrates an irony that is partially explained by the received value mixes of the different realms. In general, legislators are less receptive to the arguments of social welfare bureaucrats who are professionals than they are to the lobbying of their counterparts in the Department of

---

[8] Herbert Kaufman's *The Forest Ranger* (Baltimore: Johns Hopkins, 1963) is a classic study of this pattern.

Defense. Even within the realm of social welfare and control, one finds professionalized bureaucrats being given decidedly different receptions by legislators.

Social welfare bureaucrats may dominate and represent their clientele, but most of these groups constitute no real political threat to the electoral chances of legislators. Some clientele are diffuse, yet are so firmly attached to received values that their bureaucratic representatives are treated with the deference accorded those who represent constituencies. Social security recipients are clients who fall into this category, while AFDC mothers definitely do not. Social control bureaucrats who claim high issue saliency and who possess no clientele at all may be greeted with open arms by legislators who wish to "clean up the drug problem" or "eradicate crime in the streets." The FBI and the DEA may exist in the same realm as social workers, but the FBI's claims are likely to be accorded the respect shown admirals like Hyman Rickover and generals like Curtis LeMay during the 1950s.

Thus while it is true that professionalized bureaucrats in any realm are accorded significant amounts of deference, their allocative wishes are less likely to be acceded to by legislators when they represent clients or victims. One can, therefore, predict the likelihood of budget cuts in social welfare programs with no strong attachments to the received value mix or the self-interest of legislators. Such cuts will *destroy* existing programs only if they have been recently created (like the War on Poverty). Aggregate *reduction* in existing programs (like the food stamp program) is most likely to occur when the representing bureaucrats speak for a clientele that has no strong association with a received value and which is a remote threat to the electoral status quo.

Clientele Creation and the Elaboration of the Welfare State: 1954–1976

The realm of social welfare is by far the most extensive, qualitatively and quantitatively. It is, therefore, at the peril of exclusion that one proceeds to identify only four realms of the political within the general realm. It is difficult to think of any aspect of human behavior with which some agency of the state is not concerned. I have chosen four major contemporary items in hopes of capturing some of the interrelated causes and structures of social welfare policy. These are: race and poverty, the education explosion, internal security, and the idea of professions as constituencies.

The matter of race emerged as a significant realm of the political through the actions of organized pressure groups battling in the courts in the 1950s. The first of a series of dramas was enacted in the Supreme Court in the case of *Brown v. Board of Education* in 1954. The issue became a crisis when in 1957 President Eisenhower was forced to send federal troops to enforce an integration order in Little Rock, Arkansas, in the face of defiance by the Governor of Arkansas, Orval Faubus. This incident is significant not only because of the use of federal power in a heretofore local jurisdictional area (education). The crisis was televised nationally, thus beginning an era of troops, policemen, screaming white demonstrators, and quiet black students marching relentlessly into the livingrooms of the entire population.

From Little Rock in 1957 to Selma in 1963, the matter of racial injustice expanded the size and significance of pressure groups fighting for civil rights for blacks. By the early 1960s the realm included a variety of integrated groups engaged in marches, litigation, and lobbying. Significant national legislation was effectively blocked until the Johnson landslide of 1964. The courts and the Department of Justice became the foci for pressure from the NAACP and other groups anxious to guarantee the rights of equal access to schools, restaurants, and other public facilities. Heroic struggles against the forces of segregation, which then dominated the South, resulted in major changes in the legal and political rights of blacks. When the attention of the civil rights movement turned from political and civil injustice to economic and social inequality, the questions of class that had lain dormant in American political debate emerged with a vengeance.

By the mid-1960s it became clear to the leadership of the civil rights movement, some politicians and bureaucrats, and many social scientists that the problem was not just a legal one. Blacks constituted an underclass in rural and urban America, and they simply had not shared in the common blessings of postwar America. Blacks disproportionately lacked decent housing, nutrition, health services, education, and job opportunities possessed by millions of white Americans. From the question of civil rights to the question of economic and social deprivation was a short, albeit significant, jump.

The issue broadened as more and more institutional actors began to define the needs of blacks in economic and social terms. As in the New Deal era, the locus of power moved from the state governments to the welfare professionals in Washington. The Economic Opportunity Act of 1964 signaled the diffusion of the "black problem" to powerful institutional actors in the federal bureaucracy who engaged in elaborate efforts to create new organizational entities. The so-called poverty agencies competed with and amplified local services that were believed to be either inadequate or antithetical to the special needs of the black underclass, which had migrated in substantial numbers to the core of the big cities of the nation. A vital set of linkages between organized and unorganized blacks and the panoply of federal agencies in the social welfare realm was established and became a significant realm of the political during the last decade. The range of concerns was enormous and eventually tended to include the problems of blacks as a special subset in the realms of everything from public housing to pre-school education.[9]

The year 1957 proved to be as significant in the area of education as it was in the matter of racial politics. That was the year that the U.S.S.R. successfully launched Sputnik, the little orb that provided so many with the ammunition needed to push the federal government into the education business in a big way. The states and some localities had created some outstanding public university and college systems without a great deal of federal aid, but Sputnik ignited the fires of interest group liberalism in a number of unforeseen ways.

President Eisenhower, Congressional leaders, and the mass media saw the little satellite as a potential military threat and as evidence that American education was failing to provide the kind of skilled scientific and technical expertise that the Russians apparently had in abundance. Only God knows the reality of the "threat," but without speculating on divine knowledge, one can suggest that the pool of scientific and technological genius in America was at least adequate to the competition that the Russians were likely to present. I note in passing that the brains and talents applied to the space programs of the 1960s and 1970s in America were educated in the dark, pre-Sputnik era.

The justification for federal expansion in the area of education, of course, need not have anything to do with a putative cause of any sort,

[9] The emergence of this realm, the roles of bureaucrats and social scientists, and intrarealm politics are beautifully illustrated in Lee Rainwater and William L. Yancey, *The Moynihan Report and the Politics of Controversy* (Cambridge, Mass.: M.I.T. Press, 1967).

since this expansion was also an act of political definition. Sputnik was the convenient explanation for expansion. In point of fact, a series of powerful actors associated with public education actively solicited federal aid to enhance and expand existing programs. The Office of Education and other agencies began to develop programs to benefit nearly every kind of educational and intellectual effort one could imagine.[10]

New curricula, facilities, and scholarship aid in complex variety began to appear in the early 1960s. Americans believed that the route of upward economic and social mobility was paved with college degrees. By 1970 it had become a commonplace that education alone could perform this function. Furthermore, it was widely believed that part of the solution to social problems of all sorts could be achieved by expanding educational opportunities to all members of society.

The vast expansion of federal and state expenditures for education during the 1960s presented an unprecedented opportunity for the elaboration of profession. The development of new professional categories created the possibility of new post-secondary and graduate degree programs for colleges and universities. Government at all levels became the significant employer of professionals. Civil service requirements increasingly were drawn to exclude those who lacked the proper credentials. The number of specialized graduate degrees offered in America expanded greatly along with the universities that granted them. In this the federal government was vital, for it had become (along with large foundations) *the* financier of research and training in the universities. Universities became the most significant focal points for government service training of all sorts. Public health officials, Peace Corpsmen, nearly every Ph.D. candidate in the sciences and social sciences, CIA trainees, and potential city managers all lived on some manner of federal largesse.

The states (with the help of substantial federal aid) attempted to improve and expand the training of elementary and secondary school teachers. In doing so they helped to elaborate one of the great "guild professions" in America. State laws require teachers to hold certain mini-

---

[10] The more familiar of these programs are Head Start and Upward Bound. Others include Title III of the National Defense Education Act of 1958 (NDEA) which provided federal assistance for strengthening instruction in subjects considered "critical," such as science, math, and foreign languages. Title I of the Elementary and Secondary Education Act of 1965 (ESEA) grants aid to local educational agencies for the education of children from low-income families, and Titles II and III provide for school library resources, instructional materials, and supplementary educational centers and services. Other programs range from aid for vocational education to school lunch and milk programs.

mum qualifications before they may teach. Who determines the minima of teacher qualification? State education departments filled with Ph.D.'s in education (usually from the local state university's education program) determine the minima. Who teaches the teachers? Ph.D.'s from a state university education department teach the teachers. Education bureaucrats write curricula (lesson plans that tell teachers what their classes are to know by what date in the school year) and define the standards of admission to the profession. The unionization of teachers in the 1970s introduced further rigidities into the area of public education.

Billions have been spent on educational programs. National test scores in English and mathematics decline with seeming disregard for how much is spent. No college professor worth his salt will argue against the contention that the quality of student writing has deteriorated in the last ten years. The mediocrity of American elementary and secondary education may be debated. What may not be debated is the total control of the substance of that education by the guild profession of education. Public policy alternatives emerge from the education guild which, I hasten to add, contains a diversity of opinion. The legitimacy and significance of a given opinion, however, are a function of proper credentials and hierarchical position.

The education realm of the social welfare realm is enormous, complex, professionalized, and as frighteningly powerful in the context of its clients as any set of defense contractors or agri–businessmen. As other realms place demands on the education profession and as it seeks to maintain hegemony over its domain, it begins to take on the characteristics of the whole government of which it is a part. Administration (there are, of course, a set of special degrees in educational administration), police functions, social and psychological services, and dozens of other activities having nothing in particular to do with teaching children to read, write, and cipher now characterize large portions of educational budgets. Alternatives to the present configuration of curriculum, teacher education standards and the like must be legitimated by the guild, or they are likely to die. The education guild allocates and competes for resources within the general realm of social welfare. Of the resources garnered, the policies likely to be underwritten are not likely to be employed against the perceived best interests of the state education department, the education departments of state universities, or the teachers' unions. If the interests of the student were to diverge from those of this guild, what efficacious recourse might he or she have? Those of any client.

A third realm of the social welfare and control realm consists of the internal security forces of the nation. These are federal, state, and local policemen and administrators, plus the educational establishments, unions, and other interest groups that surround them. The 1960s saw three dramatic developments which police leadership used to enhance and expand their realm. The riots in black ghettos, protests against the war in Viet Nam during the late 1960s and the early 1970s, and the drug problem were dramatized and broadcast on television almost nightly. "Crime in the streets" and "law and order" were found to be useful issues by politicians. We have discussed the growth of the federal police agencies and need say little more except to suggest that the trends toward increased jurisdiction and a concomitant growth in size noted in the 1950s did not abate in the least. State and local police forces were expanded, and the Nixon administration created the Law Enforcement Assistance Administration to improve the quality of police services in the cities and states. Hundreds of millions of dollars disbursed by this program were used to purchase military hardware, communication devices, and training. Educational requirements of many police forces were also raised substantially during this period.

In addition to the CIA and FBI, two agencies of the federal government increased in size and significance during this period. The Internal Revenue Service first received national attention as a criminal justice agency when income tax evasion became the basis for the successful prosecution of gangster Al Capone in the 1930s. As taxation became more baroque and as the computer came into full use, the possibilities for discovering fraud and error and for instilling fear grew apace. Recently, the threat of IRS audits and the enforcement practices of the agency have come into the news, revealing the IRS as a significant federal police force. Politicians accord it the same respect that they accorded J. Edgar Hoover's notorious secret files. The discretionary power to investigate, audit, and prosecute makes the IRS a formidable agent of social control.

The Bureau of Narcotics became the Drug Enforcement Agency during this period, and extensive campaigns were launched against the plague of drugs that had come to haunt the nation. Heroin, imported from the Near East, Southeast Asia, and eventually from Mexico, was the prime target, although marijuana was to remain high on the list along with cocaine and chemicals such as LSD and methadrine. Drug enforcement has also become a much more significant element in the activities of state and local police agencies. The interrealm border skirmishes between the law enforcement realm and the health realm continue and appear to be slowly moving in favor of the health powers.

Functional organization of city and state police departments has continued along the lines suggested by the drug example. More and more police departments organize themselves in functional as well as regional units. Although this development is not new (murder, robbery, and other crimes have constituted bases for functional specialization for years), the kinds of problems serving as organizing foci have changed. The threat of civil disturbance provides another example of this. City after city was hit by civil disturbances in black neighborhoods during the 1960s. Immediately following these disturbances came protest marches, sit-ins, riots, and acts of civil disobedience directed at the war in Viet Nam. The common form of organizational response to these contingencies was the development of special units designed to show a maximum of force as soon as a disturbance broke out. There is today a newly militarized aspect to modern police forces and an increased reliance on hardware.

In addition, the police have increasingly found themselves acting in nontraditional roles. Many of the people with whom they deal are not criminals in any significant sense. It has repeatedly been found that the police function as marriage counselors, social workers, paramedics, and traffic controllers more than they function as criminal-catching coppers. Paradoxically, every increase in the number of policemen has been matched by an increase in crime; every increase in crime seems to be matched by an increase in the number of policemen.[11] Whether the police are discovering more crime as a function of their increased numbers or whether crime is increasing absolutely, one cannot say. What one can say, however, is that the discretionary acts of policemen are vital to an understanding of what kinds of behaviors are defined as arrestable.[12] Crime is discovered by policemen more among the poor, the young, and

[11] To be more precise, in the period 1970–1973, the total number of crimes increased by 7.1% while the number of policemen increased by 12.2%. See U.S. Bureau of the Census, *Statistical Abstract of the United States: 1975* (96th edition), Washington, D.C., 1975, p. 150.

	Social Welfare Realm Employees		
	1950	*1960*	*1970*
Policemen	171,200	288,520	548,000
Health service workers	410,313	735,700	1,224,900
Social service workers	48,610	94,579	216,623
Teachers	914,000	1,600,000	2,288,000

Sources: U.S. Bureau of the Census, *Census of the Population,* of the years 1950, 1960, 1970, Washington, D.C.

[12] Jerome Skolnick, *Justice Without Trial* (New York: Wiley, 1966) makes this point to good effect.

among minorities than among the not-poor, nonminorities.[13] Further-more, the chances of being convicted and incarcerated are differentially increased for the members of these groups than for any other.

The modern policeman, like the modern teacher, has a difficult and ambiguous job. He is the external, manifest, and most visible representa-tion of the power of the state; policemen are hated or applauded, de-pending upon one's experience and expectations of them. Policemen, like teachers, must in many areas deal with people and problems unrelated to their personal experience. They end up with the victims of society as they also create them. The cops transport indigents, lunatics, and deviants out of their own environments and into the hands of state institutions. In many instances the removal of drunks, maniacs, and bums to holding vats may be as much a kindness as a punishment. No policeman can ade-quately deal with the kinds of problems that such people have, and no one in the larger society can or will do much for these "unfortunates." The number and variety of these kinds of noncriminal cases have multi-plied in the present era as drugs and blight take over whole chunks of urban areas. The police are trapped in part by the same set of environ-mental circumstances as the "unfortunates."

The police are organized in paramilitary fashion and are typically socialized to sets of hierarchical and authoritarian values that cause prob-lems in dealing with populations not similarly socialized. As police salaries and professional training increase, the question of the role of the police in modern society becomes even more complex. Professionalization and unionization may increase the insularity borne of class, residential, and ethnic differences. The problems of disjunction between the police and the population they most directly confront enlarge.

The police have become powerful actors in the competition for state and local resources. Fear of crime and disorder are issues well exploited by police spokesmen at every level as they seek to increase their share of the resources allocated within the realm. Police unions have been particu-larly successful in bringing pressure to bear in many urban areas. Na-tional police organizations and powers have been expanded and am-plified to the point where one finds it difficult to discover what is *not* a federal crime. The agencies of formal social control have become more professionalized, specialized, and powerful at every level of government, and their capacity to define the set of behaviors over which they shall have hegemony grows apace.

[13] James Q. Wilson, *Varieties of Police Behavior* (New York: Atheneum, 1970) makes this point, as do many other studies.

A fourth realm contains the health professions. Unlike public school teachers and policemen, the professions populating this area have enormously powerful private allies and competitors. The state is directly involved in such public health functions as disease prevention, epidemiology, and a variety of community health services. Localities, states, and the federal government operate a wide range of general and specialized health and hospital facilities. To some extent all of these are dependent upon the services of medical practitioners who are products of the professional schools and private professional organizations which grant the right of passage into the profession. Policing is essentially a fusion of public and private power for doctors. Medicine, nursing, dentistry, and a variety of technical specialities are fully professionalized under an extraordinarily fine division of labor. Hospitals are nearly total institutions, and the professions that inform their operation are extremely hierarchical and status conscious.

Public policy regarding health care is evolving toward some sort of system of national health insurance. Medicare, Medicaid, and the various state programs under them provide benefits for the elderly and for those unable to afford private medical care and insurance. When national health insurance becomes a reality, we can expect to see a fusion of public and private power in the health field that will constitute a bureaucratic constituency of great power. The conflict and cooperation patterns beginning to emerge show all the earmarks of constituency politics. The medical professions today are major beneficiaries of government through transfer payments to individuals, institutions, and localities. The federal government has been building hospitals for a generation and has been in the business of providing total medical care for some veterans and for all military personnel and their families for longer than that. The emerging patterns of resource allocation make the bureaucracies within HEW the probable focus of increased power.

The mental health wing of the medical profession constitutes another major growth industry in the public sector. The discovery of powerful tranquilizers has enabled the mental health profession to increase institutional turnover by creating more outpatients than ever before. The retarded, the nonfunctioning mentally ill, and the elderly still abide in warehouses, however. The line between the mental health community and the law enforcement realm has blurred in recent years, and larger numbers of convicted criminals are being consigned to mental health professionals in lieu of wardens and jailors.

The mental health component of the health realm has grown along-

side its physical brother, and we are now graced with a National Institute of Health and a National Institute of Mental Health. These
powerful agencies disburse federal largesse for research and experimen-
tation to hospitals and universities across the land. The number of new
professions associated with mental health has grown in proportion to
the number and variety of physical health professions. Aides, technicians,
orderlies, nurses, social workers, and the like form the base of the important pyramid that is the mental health profession. This is amplified by
the inevitable growth and development of the health and hospital administration professions.

The provision of health services to the poor and the near-poor is not
dissimilar from the provision of other services, such as police protection
and education. Those least advantaged seem in general to be most lacking in adequate health care. Enormous sums have been spent on the
technology of medicine and on research of one sort or another; the political system is in this instance fully supportive of the state of the medical
art or science. The potential redistributive aspects of a national health
plan have tended to make one kind of public expenditure appear legitimate to the medical profession, while the other has been actively opposed.
The public monies invested in research, facilities, and the like are somehow less socialistic to the AMA than public health insurance programs,
which might reduce the economic autonomy of physicians.

The Politics of Distribution and Redistribution

Social welfare expenditures at every level of government have been
the dominant feature of budget documents during the period. The federal role in the social welfare and control realm has increased dramatically, and the politics of the past fifteen years or so have been almost
exclusively concerned with the expansion of existing services and the
provision of new ones. The lion's share of the resources in this realm lies,
of course, in "uncontrollable" expenditures. In 1966, 21.5 percent of the
federal budget went to income security programs, the most significant of
which is Social Security payments. The estimated budget outlay for 1976
is 34.0 percent of the total budget. Education, manpower, and social
services grew from a 3 percent share in 1966 to a 4.2 percent share in
1976, the peak year being 1972 when the federal government spent

5 percent of the budget in this area. Veterans' benefits and services (separate from all other categories) amounted to about 4 percent of total budgetary outlays in this period. Law enforcement grew from 0.4 percent to 0.9 percent. Lest one mistakenly believe the latter to be an insignificant amount of money, it is well to recall that this little 0.9 percent equals $3,200,000,000 (three point two billion dollars).[14]

The politics of social welfare is the politics of distribution and redistribution.[15] The working population of the nation pays the bills of those who cannot or will not generate their own sources of support. Social Security payments to retirees who contributed throughout their lives to the program are in excess of their contributions because Congress has consistently voted increases reflecting inflationary changes. Even so, Social Security payments are barely adequate. The fund may be actuarially unsound to boot, meaning that people are living longer than anticipated when the resource base was initially calculated in the 1930s. In addition, Medicare for the aged and Medicaid for low-income people now cost the taxpayer approximately $26 billion annually. One segment of the population is to an ever-increasing degree paying for the medical, educational, retirement, and general living costs of another part of the population. The balance tips annually in favor of the nonproductive population and the burden of taxation grows with it. The states are locked into the same kinds of uncontrollable spending programs.

Programs are uncontrollable for fairly obvious legal and political reasons.[16] Millions of people would live in more highly restricted circumstances if such programs were to be discontinued or seriously curtailed. Medical care would be unavailable to many in need. No politician or bureaucrat without a serious death wish can think of backing away from the implied promise that is Social Security, Medicaid, and Medicare. One simply does not stay in office by chucking grandma and grandpa into the street. After all, grandma and grandpa spent a not inconsiderable amount of *their* income on a Social Security fund for their retirement, and

[14] Office of Management and Budget, *The United States Budget in Brief, 1976* (Washington, D.C.: Government Printing Office, 1976), p. 50.

[15] See Theodore Lowi's "American Business, Public Policy, Case-Studies, and Political Theory," *World Politics* (July, 1964), 677–715 for an interesting identification of governmental policies as being distributive, regulatory, or redistributive.

[16] Martha Derthick, *Uncontrollable Spending for Social Service Grants* (Washington, D.C.: The Brookings Institution, 1975) is an excellent case study of the bureaucratic politics and bumbling of grants-in-aid to the states under the public assistance sections of the Social Security Act.

they justifiably feel entitled to getting their dollars back. The tragedy is that those dollars are inflated, and so the old folks need a bit more than they put in. The dollars I spend on Social Security simply will not be there in 2005 when I retire, because they must be spent on people retiring before then.

Once a program is established and is widely believed to provide an indispensable/no-alternative service, spending for it becomes uncontrollable. Once such a program is in place and carries with it *guaranteed minimum benefits,* then *revenue* becomes the problem, since thought about expenditure is all but precluded. There are many persons and institutions wholly dependent upon government support for their existences; hospitals, schools, nursing homes, and the like are often in a position analogous to that of the Social Security beneficiary. If we look at the "uncontrollables" as a given, a base which is unlikely to be contested by anyone, then wherein lies the politics of social welfare?

The politics of this realm are to be discovered at the margins of uncontrollable spending. Increases and expansions of programs with direct benefits to individuals are likely to occur as a result of a kind of constituency politics that is very different from the kind of politics discussed in the realm of political economy. While electoral politicians attempt to discover new areas of "subjective indispensability" in their constituents, it is within the configurations of the social welfare and control realms that truly potent constituencies are to be discovered. These large, formal, and professionalized bureaucratic entities represent their own vital interests when they propose program expansions. The realms of the police, teachers, doctors, and welfare workers differ substantially, but in certain key political aspects they share common features.

The most prominent feature of each of these realms is their dependence upon government resources for existence and expansion; there is no other source of support. The route of upward career mobility for most people (excepting physicians) in the four realms is within the context of some formal public organization. The more programs, the more supervisory personnel needed. The more supervisory personnel, the more hierarchical slots available for advancement. Empire-building of this sort is further complicated by professionalism. While empire-building is a commonplace in all large organizations, those public social welfare organizations with large, professional memberships are likely to be subject to a particular form of growth that is peculiarly significant to the political process.

Technological changes in professionalized fields like medicine and education are likely to be accompanied by demands for new professionals, equipment, and resources, which are grounded in politically sensitive realities. The introduction of a new therapeutic, educational, or criminal detection technique or machine will probably bring a demand for its uniform national deployment.[17] Such a demand, based in part on equity, altruism, and self-interest, is in some ways simple to understand. If I introduce high-level intensive care technology in one public hospital and can show benefits to patients who need the technology, what is the justification for not deploying it throughout all public hospitals in the nation? Or, how can one be properly educated without some instruction in computer use and technology? The installation of the machinery and the manpower to staff it become virtually mandatory for the educational institution desiring to "keep up." Legislators may say "no" to such demands on the basis of an insufficiency of funds, but they are not likely to challenge the claim on grounds of superior competency within the field.

Structuring alternatives in the case of highly professionalized social welfare bureaucrats is at least as significant as the alternative-structuring behavior of economists. Indeed, it may be even more significant, because of the interesting kind of politics typifying this realm. Clients and victims, it will be remembered, are distinguished by the limited potential control they have over the agents of the state upon which they depend. Hospital patients, the elderly, poor, students, indigents, the mentally ill, and criminals have few, if any, resources with which to effectively counter policies with which they disagree. In no significant way is the future of the government actor likely to be altered by the client's behavior—exactly the reverse of those actors charged with regulating unions, banks, and large industries. Clients are unorganized by virtue of their clienthood. To be a client is to be a single entity, faced with the uniform, regularized rules of the dispensing agency and having no serious recourse to altering those rules.

The political crux of clienthood is in the use that the true constituents of the social welfare and control realm put to it. Those who exercise constituency-like power in this realm are the organized and often union-

---

[17] A major theoretical claim which supports this statement and goes well beyond it is Jacques Ellul, *The Technological Society* (New York: Vintage, 1964). Interesting arguments and cases appear in Todd R. LaPorte, *Organized Social Complexity* (Princeton: Princeton University Press, 1975); see particularly Jennifer Nias, "The Sorcerer's Apprentice: A Case Study of Complexity in Educational Institutions," p. 256.

ized members of the large, public social welfare bureaucracies. As in the case of unions and other large-scale aggregations of interest, the desires of the elites who manage are preeminent in the realm. These elites are conscious of the norms and prerogatives of public professional life and now must also be cognizant of the demands of unionized members of the organization they direct.

Two sources of constituent-like pressure emerge from public social welfare bureaucracy. One source of power comes from the managerial elites who command not only the normal resources of large organizations, but who also claim to represent the interests of the clients of those organizations. Thus, *the constituency is the organization itself,* and one of its resources is the claim that it is the significant representative of its clientele. Claims for improving education always rest on the argument that the suggested improvements are for the ultimate benefit of the students. Patients, welfare recipients, and so on are similarly employed. Claims about what would or would not benefit the client and victim poor are seldom made by them. When they are made, they are seldom heard.

Attempts at turning the poor into a true constituency were made during the War on Poverty period, and much sound and fury were heard during the 1960s about people "having a say in the decisions that affect their lives." Actually, such attempts at organizing a clientele to look like a constituency were very often entrepreneurial bureaucratic efforts at domain expansion.[18] He who funds his clients can often make them appear to others as constituents. But *effective power cannot be simply granted in this realm, since the recipient has no effective way of retaining it should the donor change his mind.*

Clientele, then, can be a significant resource, if its representatives can convince other powerful actors that it has some of the aspects of constituency. In the cases of victim-centered public welfare and control organizations, appeals and demands are nearly impossible to make, for it is extraordinarily difficult to make prisoners, inmates, or alcoholics appear to be constituents. Victim-centered agencies must look to other avenues for authenticating their claims on resources. The police use public relations techniques that are directed at funding agencies fearful of public reaction to crime scares. Mental institutions and the like have little effective claimant power grounded in constituency or public relations. They also receive comparatively few resources.

[18] Daniel Patrick Moynihan, *Maximum Feasible Misunderstanding* (New York: Free Press, 1969).

A second and in many ways dissonant source of power from the social welfare realm is the unionization of public employees.[19] It is within the realm of social welfare and control that most government employees (exclusive of the military) are to be found. It is also this realm that has experienced the most aggressive and thorough unionization. Teachers, policemen, hospital workers, clerical personnel, and almost every occupational category that is not managerial has been unionized. Government employees in these areas have thus become a significant force independent of the agency for which they work. Unionization has increased the cost of public welfare functions dramatically in the past five years, and there is every reason to expect that such costs will continue to rise. Job descriptions become increasingly rigid, and working conditions improve. Public employees' benefit and retirement plans have become a significant cost of operation on the state and local level. Indeed, the teachers' unions momentarily "bailed out New York City" during its recent fiscal embarrassment by redirecting the investment choices of union pension funds temporarily.

Public sector union leadership has one outstanding and commonly shared value with the managerial elite directing bureaucratic action in the specific realms of social welfare: There is deep consensus on the need to keep and expand social welfare programs and employment. Without jobs there is no union. Without jobs there is less program and perhaps less need for managers. Public sector employees now constitute *the* formidable organized electoral force in some cities, and one can expect an increase in their participation in political campaigns. Teachers, policemen, sanitation men, and hospital workers, united with administrators in common cause, make for a potentially staggering political force in the battle for resource allocation.

Beneath the political power of empire-builders, expertise, monopolis-

[19] The number and size of public employee unions escalated so rapidly during the 1960s and early 1970s that it is difficult to obtain accurate figures for them. Sterling D. Spero and John M. Capozzola in their *The Urban Community and Its Unionized Bureaucracies* (New York: Dunellen, 1973) estimate that in 1968 there were 1,160 major public employee unions in the country. A Bureau of Labor Statistics report of 1971 estimates that 2,317,000 government workers are members of public employee organizations. The 111% increase in the membership of the American Federation of State, County, and Municipal Employees (AFSCME) from 1960 to 1970 is a clear demonstration of the scale of growth these unions are experiencing. See BLS, *Municipal Employee Associations,* August, 1971. The Contract Research Corporation's *Public Sector Labor Relations: An Evaluation of Policy-Related Research* (NSF Contract #WSF-3838, February, 1975) is a monumental study of public employee unionism.

tic control, technological diffusion, constituency-like representation, and unionization lies a perhaps more basic reason for the emergence of the social welfare and control realm as the preeminent recipient of public resources. The payments and services provided by the social welfare realm are among the most subjectively indispensable and immediate of government actions. Since the Great Depression there has been a consistent drift toward widespread belief in government as the supplier of last resort. This notion is reflected in the commonly held belief that those unable to buy services like health care should have them provided by government. As our expectations and the costs of medical care have increased, so too has our belief that all should be entitled to it. Problems that were once understood to be either bad luck or the responsibility of the family have come to be viewed as matters of public concern, and the range and extent of social welfare functions expand accordingly. The elderly and the provision of their needs have been transformed from the specialized problem of the destitute to the general problem of most members of the social order. The care and support of the elderly are now an enormous public and commercial business, because people believe that they cannot or should not handle the matter through their personal resources. Old age homes and nursing homes dependent upon direct or indirect government subsidy are not filled exclusively with the parents of the poor.

Every realm within the general realm of social welfare has willingly had its functions and personnel expanded. The combination of political/ bureaucratic entrepreneurship and subjective indispensability is unbeatable. The political link becomes tenuous as one searches in vain for evidence of public control of client and victim-centered agencies of the state. Problem children are now as much the province of the schools and their associated noneducational services as they are of the nuclear family. That family, we hear repeatedly, is fast disappearing in the maelstrom of industrialization; its members disperse to become clients of the state. The overlap of clientele of the police, welfare workers, hospitals, asylums, and nursing homes grows as people generally come to accept the idea that what were personal and familial problems are now best dealt with by state agencies. The population of "unfortunates" has now grown to include more of us than ever before. The abject, anomic, helpless in our midst no longer are confined to institutions only *in extremis*. Their growing numbers have come to include an ever expanding set of categories of deviance.

The poor, it has been too frequently noted, are always with us. I discussed relative deprivation and the conversion of wants into needs in chapter two. During this era some real progress was made in the area of income poverty,[20] yet the problems of poverty, illiteracy, and malnutrition continue to haunt us. The poor are disproportionately arrested, convicted, and incarcerated, especially the black poor. Black and white poor are disproportionately represented in combat units of the peacetime armed forces, just as they were in the pre-volunteer Viet Nam War armed forces. One has but to name a stigma, and one can discover the poor disproportionately represented in the institutional population.

At the moment race and poverty have left the public agenda of electoral politicians, and middle-class welfare continues as ever to dominate the social welfare realm. There are millions of middle- and upper-middle class children attending public colleges and universities, despite their parents' ability to pay the full costs of their education. Real estate hustlers continue to dominate the urban housing market in poor neighborhoods, as HUD plows millions into guaranteeing mortgages that will never be paid off because the housing is unfit for habitation and grows worse as it is abandoned.

The politics of social welfare and control are the politics of large, formal professionalized organizations acting as the representatives of their own interests and the interests of the clientele which depend upon them. No politically significant organizations oppose the representations of the social welfare bureaucracies as to the needs of their clientele. Such representations in the forms of demands and claims are clothed in the jargon of profession and legitimated by the politicians who accept them. The social welfare and control realm successfully competes for the allocation of scarce public resources in institutional and mass media forums. It is seldom directly assaulted in electoral contests. The relationship between the swelling population of more or less permanent clients and the democratic norms that allegedly limit and direct social welfare agencies of the state is increasingly problematic. No theory of the state has yet to account for the subordination of the citizen who becomes a client. No effective means of political linkage between the client and those who manage the clientele exists. And those who are victims continue to be completely outside common political discourse, in large measure because they are unable to claim any participatory role whatsoever.

While it is painfully obvious that expectations of what social welfare

[20] Robert Plotnick and Felicity Skidmore, *Progress Against Poverty* (New York: Academic Press, 1975).

agencies can do have been raised to almost dangerous levels, the causes of such elevation are not entirely clear. Certainly, agencies of the state and politicians have led people to believe in the possibility that government can provide happiness and security for all. It is equally true that expectations rise independent of state action or promise. They rise as a function of subjective indispensability and of relative deprivation in the social and economic order. The common equalizer, the great rectifier, has for several generations been understood to be the state. Recently, a few politicians have attempted to suggest that the state is limited in what it can do, but I understand their argument to be essentially an economic one: The average middle-income wage earner already gives his total earnings for the months of January, February, March, April, and part of May to the state in one form of taxation or another.

Ironies abound. As one becomes a client, one loses power to alter the outcomes of the agency that affects his life; he surrenders effective redress by placing himself at the mercy of professional wisdom and power. As we expand services, we seem to contract liberty. Ideas that begin as liberating become bureaucratized and stultifying as they become routinized into day-to-day operation. Individual autonomy is expanded at the cost of increased dependency. Every irony becomes a potential source of intrarealm conflict through contradiction, it would seem. The contradictions within this realm, however, seldom become the source of conflict and change, because a nearly complete oligopoly dominates those who could be the major source of change—the clients and victims.

chapter five

The Realm
of National Defense

Introduction

More than any other, the realm of national defense resembles an entire social, economic, and political system. It intervenes directly and indirectly in the domestic economy and is a major buyer and seller of goods and services in the world economy. It absorbs and manipulates huge amounts of land, labor, capital, technology, and natural resources. It operates a social welfare structure on a par with many nations by providing educational services, elaborate health care facilities, a vast pension and welfare system, and a complete criminal justice apparatus. It is one of the great underwriters of scientific and technological enterprise in the world's history and contains the most complex, expensive, and sophisticated managerial systems ever devised. It is also the single most potentially destructive force on the globe.

It is the only political realm discussed so far which has a clear institutional focus and mission relatively uncomplicated by the jurisdictional problems of a federal system. At the center of the realm is the Department of Defense (DOD) which is formally and literally an organization, but one of such size and complexity as to make the term almost inadequate. The transcendent purpose and benefit of DOD are easily stated: Deterrence of enemy aggression is a public good that benefits all members of society. The ultimate output of DOD is this indivisible and objectively indispensable public good.

One benefits, then, from the national defense realm as a citizen by having his very life protected. One benefits as a constituent if the addition or withdrawal of his goods, services, or support can cause some actors in the realm to alter their allocative actions in his favor. One is a client if the realm provides him with a good or service without which he would suffer and if he has little or no influence on allocative decisions. Finally, one may be victimized by the realm in nearly every way discoverable in modern society, from incarceration in a military prison to psychiatric stigmatization to impoverishment through policy or rule change. The constituents, clients, and victims of the defense realm can be discovered throughout the world and are embodied in persons, organizations, and even nations.

The analysis of this realm differs from those in the preceding chapters in several ways and for several reasons. First and most important, many aspects of this realm are, I believe, precursors of an evolving bureaucratic state. Not only does the realm contain all the bureaucratic constituency, client, and victim relationships that I have found descriptive of modern citizenship, but it also is the best single example of the modern fusion of political power, formal organization, and professionalized expertise.

Another important difference in this realm lies in the extent to which its most political significant actors are conceived of as managers of change and interaction. Each realm discussed thus far has contained descriptions of problem-defining and problem-oriented professions and hierarchies that have developed in the recent past. Nowhere has this conception of political, social, and economic reality gained greater currency than in DOD. Political questions become managerial problems inside DOD. As powerful actors outside the realm define conditions like pollution and natural resource depletion as political problems in the future, they, too, are likely to reach for managerial solutions.

The distinction between political questions and managerial solutions employing differentially valued expertise is blurred more effectively and thoroughly in DOD than in any other organization with which I am familiar. This is not to suggest that America is imminently to become more militarized than it is or that the specific techniques of DOD are immediately applicable to other political matters. Rather, I believe that managerial and technological ideologies, removed from the traditional processes of congressional and electoral decision making, will characterize the future of American politics.

The realm of national defense is discussed not only in terms of its received values, politics, and constituents, but it is also conceived of as a rough prototype of our future. Accordingly, my focus is more on *intra-*

organizational actions than was the case in the two preceding chapters. This emphasis requires a choice from among the many systems of action discoverable in the realm. One might look at the political economy of defense or the social welfare aspects of the realm as in the Veterans' Administration. My choice is a case of weapons procurement which I believe exemplifies many significant aspects of the realm and of the bureaucratic state of the future.

Civilian Control, Science and Technology as Weapons, and Pax Americana: 1953–1961

The profession of the career military officer suggests that the best information, the most detached view, and the most intimate familiarity with conditions of potential combat lie in military thought.[1] Civilian appointees and presidents are transitory figures, yet they are due respect and obedience. The ancient dilemma is thus posed: What do laymen know or understand of war compared to professional warriors? Democratic political systems are still churning over the problem, but it suffices to say that issues of strategic planning have seldom been decided by civilians except in extreme situations.

What are the implications and reasons for this? Clearly, the politician's insecurity in the face of profession is highly significant. Military leaders are powerful and highly politicized bureaucrats who have independent linkages to sources of power external to civilian appointees. To choose strategy is to imply technologies, both mechanical and organizational. To choose technologies is to alter career patterns and possibilities.[2]

[1] Samuel Huntington brilliantly isolates and describes *officership as a profession.* He identifies the officer corps as both a bureaucratic profession and a bureaucratic organization. He understands the idea of profession in traditional terms: expertise, corporateness, and responsibility. He agrees with Lasswell's statement to the effect that the central skill of the officer corps is "the management of violence" and goes on to say that "the direction, operation, and control of a human organization whose primary function is the application of violence is the peculiar skill of the officer." Samuel P. Huntington, *The Soldier and the State* (Cambridge, Mass.: Harvard University Press, 1957), p. 11.

[2] Shifting technologies means reducing the appropriateness of painfully acquired skills and destroying the possibilities for command which are so vital to upward mobility. The point is made elegantly in Elting E. Morison, *Man, Machines, and Modern Times* (Cambridge, Mass.: M.I.T. Press, 1966), Chapter 2, "Gunfire at Sea: A Case Study of Innovation."

Such alterations upset, distress, and undermine the morale of careerists. The optimal solution to this dilemma of choice is to "choose everything" by developing a strategic doctrine that involves the capacity to respond to military threats from any source.

This hypothetical and impossible choice solves two problems. It meets the optimal needs for defending the nation and its allies, and it insures the career possibilities of the officer corps. It is a most appealing political argument. Who is for less than total national defense?

The interests of the career military are quite comprehensible in conventional bureaucratic terms. But there are other realms within the general one which benefit from this "optimal solution." Permanent civil servants in the DOD are nearly as dependent upon expanding missions and technologies as the military. They benefit in the obvious and familiar ways of hierarchical ascension. Defense contractors and some congressmen would, one expects, be equally delighted with the consequences of an optimal strategy that would defend us against any possible aggressor(s) and that involved the development of all possible organizational and mechanical technologies.

Scarcity of resources is the realistic empirical condition, however, and it inevitably leads to the conflict and cooperation activities that are the stuff of politics. Prior to the mid-1950s, the classic patterns of interservice rivalry over the allocation of scarce public resources in the national defense realm had primarily to do with missions, force levels, and hardware.[3] The president set a budget ceiling for the services and then let them fight it out among themselves. Major technological change resulting in serious organizational consequences occurred infrequently. The employment of aircraft as a major weapons system is undoubtedly the single best case of serious organizational dislocation during that time. The Army Air Force became the United States Air Force following World War II, thus creating a whole new set of career possibilities for military pilots. The Navy retained and increased its air arm. Despite these significant changes, however, the missions and weapons systems that had traditionally pertained to each service remained relatively secure.

---

[3] As Charles J. Hitch points out, efforts at reducing interservice rivalry did not end with the formation of DOD, but continued unabated until a very energetic, intelligent, and powerful group of civilians renewed the assault with limited success. See *Decision-Making for Defense* (Berkeley: University of California Press, 1965), pp. 3–21. Hitch views interservice rivalry as an historical phenomenon of great durability whose attendant costs are enormous.

Two events of major consequence occurred after the Korean War which were to upset and transform the traditional politics of the realm. The first of these was the cold war. The foreign policies of the Truman and Eisenhower years have been described and analyzed in a vast historical and social science literature.[4] Our concern is with the fact that political and military leaders believed that there was a real international danger posed by the policies and actions of aggressive communist nations. An unsatisfying conclusion to the Korean War had been reached, and the conventional wisdom in the Pentagon and in public forums was that the U.S.S.R. and the People's Republic of China constituted military threats roughly analogous to those posed by the Axis powers prior to 1939. There was, therefore, widespread agreement that failure to contain communist powers throughout the world was likely to lead to a third world war. A strategy of global deterrence seemed to be required.

This central tenet of belief established in the Truman administration was elaborated and embroidered by subsequent administrations, but the thrust remained the same until the disasterous Viet Nam War. One can only speculate about the continuation or alteration of that posture, but certain elements seem to remain. America, it is believed, was the bulwark of all noncommunist nations against conquests of all sorts, including outright invasion, internal subversion through propaganda, assassination and bribery, and wars of national liberation. America was to be prepared to defend itself and its allies against any threat. This ever-ready global strategy provided the military services with unparalleled peacetime opportunities. The military draft and the reserves remained. New bases were spread around the world. Treaties were signed guaranteeing the *pax americana*. Old enemies became new friends, although they were stimulated to revivify without armaments.[5] Nations friendly to America were generously supplied with arms. The military became a significant peacetime political actor in all of this.

---

[4] Included in the literature are George F. Kennan, *American Diplomacy 1900–1950* (Chicago: University of Chicago Press, 1951); Henry A. Kissinger, *Nuclear Weapons and Foreign Policy* (New York: Harper & Row, 1957); Gabriel Kolko, *The Roots of American Foreign Policy* (Boston: Beacon Press, 1967); Hans J. Morgenthau, *Politics Among Nations,* 4th ed. (New York: Knopf, 1967); John Spanier, *American Foreign Policy Since World War II,* 6th ed. (New York: Praeger, 1973); Robert Strausz-Hupe and others, *Protracted Conflict* (New York: Harper & Row, 1959).

[5] Indicators of post-war growth and prosperity in Germany and Japan compared to those in the U.S., U.K., and U.S.S.R. might lead one to wonder about who won World War II.

The global strategy, however, could never be supported by sufficient conventional resources to meet its implications, because total peacetime preparedness would bankrupt the nation. The resources needed to combat multiple enemies in multiple theaters of operation over an extended period of time would require expenditures approximating peak World War II levels.[6] (In 1945, 83% of the federal budget had been spent on defense. This constituted 38% of the gross national product.) The commitments implied by *pax americana* simply could not be mustered, and suboptimal solutions were devised that involved arming allies and other tactics.

The crucial ingredient, however, lay in the increased destructive power of high-technology weapons systems. The dramatic increase in the productivity of destructive force began when the nuclear weapon, the supersonic jet aircraft, and the guided missile were fused into man–machine systems. Enemies could be reached rapidly and with terrifyingly thorough effect. By the mid-1950s strategic doctrine had moved away from standing armies and navies of large size. The new doctrines involved "massive retaliation" with long-range weapons systems (Strategic Air Command bombers, submarine-launched missiles, ground-to-ground ICBMs, and carrier-launched aircraft). This new view of global war became the political and strategic conventional wisdom of the mid-1950s. Two major problems had to be solved if the doctrine was to be put into effect.

The first of these problems involved procurement. The ideas were there; the weapons were not. The state had to provide and create a set of idea, design, engineering, and procurement systems as tools for doing the job. No longer could manufacturers be presented with a set of specifications that could be readily met. Standardization of major weapons like bombers and tanks had permitted industrial concerns relatively easy conversion routines. Thus, an automotive manufacturer of decent size could (in pre–Korean War days) build plants or convert old ones to produce tanks or other military vehicles without much risk. Design and engineering problems were readily controlled. The demand for the product and the supply of labor and materials for its production were stable. Capitalization through commercial channels or some combination of government

[6] Defense spending dropped after every war, but never to pre-war levels. Bruce M. Russett, *What Price Vigilance?* (New Haven: Yale University Press, 1970), Chapter 1, "Climbing High into the Sun?"

and bank loans was not very difficult. But no shipyard had ever built nuclear submarines. The electronics of surveillance required by such systems and their subsystems either did not exist or were on drawing boards. There were abundant material resources available for production mobilization. The key resource, however, was not immediately available to the Pentagon. The technological, scientific, and managerial skills were not to be found in the military establishment of 1953.

A most prescient statement of the dilemma was discovered by Gabriel Kolko and comes from an unexpected source. In 1946, when he served as Chief of Staff of the Army, General Eisenhower wrote a memorandum on scientific and technological resources as military assets. The memo is long but of great significance. Eisenhower made five general points:

1. *The Army must have civilian assistance in military planning as well as for the production of weapons.*
2. *Scientists and industrialists must be given the greatest possible freedom to carry out their research.*
3. *The possibility of utilizing some of our industrial and technological resources as organic parts of our military structure in time of emergency should be carefully examined.*
4. *Within the army we must separate responsibility for research and development from the functions of procurement, purchase, storage, and distribution.*
5. *Officers of all arms and services must become fully aware of the advantages which the army can derive from the close integration of civilian talent with military plans and developments.*

. . . The association of military and civilians in educational institutions and industry will level barriers, engender mutual understanding, and lead to the cultivation of friendships invaluable for future cooperation. The realization of our objectives places upon us, the military, the challenge to make professional officers the equals in training and knowledge of civilians in similar fields and make our professional environment as inviting as those outside.

On January 17, 1961, President Eisenhower went on TV and radio to give his farewell address as president. In this speech he came as close as any of his predecessors to pointing out a realm of the political as I have defined it. Contrast the following description from this famous speech with the memorandum above.

Our military organization today bears little relation to that known by any of my predecessors in peacetime, or indeed by the fighting men of World War II and Korea.

Until the latest of our world conflicts, the United States had no armaments industry. American makers of plowshares could, with time and as required, make swords as well. But now we can no longer risk emergency improvisations of national defense; we have been compelled to create a permanent arms industry of vast proportions. Added to this, 3.5 million men and women are directly engaged in the Defense Establishment. We annually spend on military security more than the net income of all United States corporations.

This conjunction of an immense Military Establishment and a large arms industry is new in the American experience. The total influence— economic, political, even spiritual—is felt in every city, every statehouse, every office of the Federal Government. We recognize the imperative need for this development. Our toils, resources, and livelihood are all involved; so is the very structure of our society.

In the councils of government we must guard against the acquisition of unwarranted influence whether sought or unsought, by the military–industrial complex. [Emphasis mine.] *The potential for the disastrous rise of misplaced power exists and will persist.*

We must never let the weight of this combination endanger our liberties or democratic processes. We should take nothing for granted. Only an alert and knowledgeable citizenry can compel the proper meshing of the huge industrial and military machinery of defense with our peaceful methods and goals so that security and liberty may prosper together.

Akin to and largely responsible for the sweeping changes in our industrial–military posture has been the technological revolution during recent decades. In this revolution research has become central; it also becomes more formalized, complex, and costly. A steadily increasing share is conducted for, by, or at the direction of the Federal Government.

Today the solitary inventor, tinkering in his shop, has been overshadowed by task forces of scientists in laboratories and testing fields. In the same fashion the free university, historically the fountainhead of free ideas and scientific discovery, has experienced a revolution in the conduct of research. Partly because of the costs involved, a Government contract becomes virtually a substitute for intellectual curiosity. For every old blackboard there are now hundreds of new electronic computers.

The prospect of domination of the nation's scholars by Federal employment, project allocations, and the power of money is ever present and gravely to be regarded.

Yet in holding scientific research and discovery in respect, as we should, we must also be alert to the equal and opposite danger that public policy could itself become the captive of a scientific technological elite. [*Emphasis mine.*]

It is the task of statesmanship to mold, to balance, and to integrate these and other forces, new and old, within the principles of our democratic system—ever aiming toward the supreme goals of our free society.

These two documents cogently summarize the problem, its solution, and the negative consequences flowing from it. From Korea onward, the problem has been consistently defined in terms of the maintenance of strategic and tactical superiority over the Russians and Chinese at almost any cost. Since the dawn of the atomic age the clear way of gaining superiority has been through heavy investment in the development and manufacture of weapons systems more advanced and more numerous than those of our potential enemies. The economic power of the Pentagon and its constituents in American business, commerce, and labor has been amplified by the scientific and technological elites of the universities. Mutual co-optation has been the order of the day. Eisenhower the general and Eisenhower the president predicted it, encouraged it, and ended public life worrying about it.

Following the Korean War, conventionally defined politics in this realm have had to do with classic constituency relationships and with the development of new linkages between traditional structures of power and emerging bureaucratic elites.

Conventional constituency politics revolving around presidential campaigns and congressional representation of local interests are reasonably familiar and need only brief recapitulation. Defense contractors and an expanding domestic military presence set the stage for conflict and cooperation over the locational and economic benefits of national security. High position in House or Senate committees involves the potential ability to pour resources into one's state or district. The late Congressman L. Mendel Rivers of Charleston, S.C., who was Chairman of the House Armed Services Committee, is an extreme example of the well-known phenomenon. By 1970 his district had one Air Force base, one Army depot, a Navy shipyard, a Marine air station, a Marine recruit center, a weapons station, and a Polaris submarine training and operation center. Congressman Rivers' campaign slogan was "Rivers delivers." There were probably few people past their teen years who didn't know what it was that he delivered. Given the following, Rivers' position in the Congressional committee hierarchy thoroughly explains his ability to benefit his district:[7]

. . . In fact the budget recommended by the Department of Defense is affected very slightly by Congressional debate. Congressional reductions in defense funding proposals over the two decades 1950–1970 often amounted to less than 2%. Between 1961 and 1971 the reduction was always less than 5%, with the exception of 1970 when it reached 7%. In 1970 lengthy hearings and debate in both chambers of Congress led to a reduction of only 3%.

Those in Congress who view their appropriations, policy, and oversight responsibilities in a truly critical light were (and are) constantly faced with technological complexity that is nigh impossible to penetrate. The volume of research and development requests for funding during the late 1950s and early 1960s was matched by an increasingly complicated technological jargon and was compounded by secrecy rituals. Even when senators like Proxmire are able to penetrate the jargon and propaganda of Pentagon representatives so as to reveal scandalous cost overruns or unnecessary weapons development schemes, they are often stymied by secrecy rituals. Secrecy in Congressional hearings and in the Pentagon begins, of course, from a premise that knowledge of American weapons development and procurement plans is of great potential value to our enemies. Despite the unsavory tincture of the phrase brought on by the Watergate infamy, there *are* reasonable "national security interests." However, no one has as yet disentangled these interests from the propensity of any advocate (or incompetent) to cloak his cause or his errors in this reasonable censorship. Congressmen and senators are faced with some serious dilemmas when they oppose Pentagon actions.

How does one decide that revelation is injurious to national security? How does one attempt to overcome the natural advantages of profession-

[7] J. Ronald Fox, *Arming America* (Cambridge: Harvard University Press, 1974), pp. 126, 150.

alized expertise in order to combat the development of yet another high-technology weapons system? How does one deal with the natural inclination of one's colleagues to support programs that are obviously going to benefit constituencies and reelection campaigns? No single answer to such questions is to be found in the halls of Congress. The Pentagon defines the rules of the decisional game in enough ways to dominate it.[8]

[8] Fox, *Arming America,* cites five "games" employed by the Pentagon to achieve funding for endangered programs. He claims that he saw each practiced at least twice during his four years in DOD. I believe them significant enough to cite in full (pp. 136–137).

Game #1: Our friends on the Senate staff tell us that committee members believe we have spent too much on research and development for Program X. They say we are not likely to obtain additional funds, even though the R&D tasks are still incomplete. To take care of this problem, we will redefine the remaining work as Advanced Production Engineering, thereby giving Congress the idea that production is underway. This strategy will work because we asked for, and obtained, some APE funds last year, before we found that the program was not yet ready to enter production. If we *don't* ask for APE funds this year, we lose out on two counts. First, we won't obtain the funds we need to continue R&D. Second, we raise a red flag that something is wrong because they will be expecting a request for either R&D or APE funds. No request may mean an end to the entire program.

Game #2: Congressman A has requested specific information on the cost and capability of System B, but there is no law that says we have to give it to him. System B is in hot water right now and we'd rather not have him know what is happening just before budget hearings. The committee chairman, who doesn't like troublemakers either, has told us "off the record" to ignore the Congressman's request. We have two choices. We can drag our feet and delay the submission of the data, or we can present the Congressman with so much detail that he will never figure out what is happening. His staff is small, and it would take them six months to go through the masses of data we could provide.

Game #3: Although a majority of the Senate committee does not support us on this budget request, there is no real cause for alarm. The House has given us strong backing and the Senate chairman is also behind us. In fact, he has told us that he will not bring the issue to a head in his own committee because he can arrange to have the item restored by the joint Senate–House Conference Committee. We know from experience that we can depend on him.

Game #4: Congressman Z has us over a barrel. He has warned us that he will see that funds are not appropriated for our two most important programs unless we scrap our plans to close the military base in his district. It will cost us $10 million a year to keep the base open, and we don't need it at all. But it looks as though this is the price we will have to pay to get the funds we want for these two programs.

Presidential campaigns during the period under discussion could have done nothing but delight Pentagon expansionists. As he suggests in his own memoranda and speeches, Eisenhower contributed his earnest support to the growth of the expanding Pentagon about which he later came to worry. The supreme irony of the 1960 presidential campaign was the great "missile gap" nonsense. Kennedy publicized and ran on a spurious argument, suggesting that America was falling behind the Russians in the production of ICBMs. His foreign policy speeches and those of his opponent stressed the need for a "strong national defense." Since it continues to be difficult to discover candidates in favor of a weak national defense, how seriously is the claim to be taken?

The claim becomes more than the usual campaign effluvia when it gets converted into part of a belief system that understands foreign policy and domestic economic reality as being grounded in the defense industry. Kennedy was (through the missile gap rhetoric) assuring unions, workers, businessmen, bankers, and foreign client nations that if he were elected, they could expect not only a continuation but an expansion of the Eisenhower policies.

The politics and policies of the 1950s in the national defense realm revolved around an expansion of military power throughout the political system. This was coupled with growing economic interdependencies and a new and permanent military role for technological change and its management. The latter occurred not only in the Pentagon and in its evolving industrial clients and constituents, but also in universities and private consulting firms. Because constituents and clients have organizational as well as individual personifications, it is important to suggest that the realm was expanded and elaborated by the presence of these new actors in the 1950s and early 1960s.

Private consulting firms such as the RAND Corporation (an Air Force child that matured into a private operation) sprung up during the period to provide the Pentagon with the brain power and expertise for

---

Game #5: Never give false statistics, but be selective with statistics that will support arguments for increased spending. If we want more ships, indicate that a potential enemy has more ships than the United States. Don't mention that U.S. ships are larger or have greater firepower. Or, talk about inferior troop strength in NATO—only 20 divisions compared to 100 Warsaw Pact divisions. Don't mention that a Russian troop division is about one-fifth the size of a U.S. troop division, or that an American division's firepower is greater than the firepower of 5 Russian divisions.

strategic and tactical planning.[9] Weapons systems, scenarios for planning military operations, economic impact of alternate weapons systems and force deployments, and literally thousands of other praxiological matters became a lucrative business for private consultants and for university faculties. Scientific and technological intellects were systematically purchased, and institutions benefited enormously through plant expansion and compensation for personnel and overhead. This involvement began in the Eisenhower years and was greatly expanded during the Kennedy–Johnson period.

The beneficiaries of Pentagon largesse at institutional and individual levels were thus discoverable throughout the social order by 1961. The politics and policies of the realm could in one sense be understood in classic pluralist terms. Name a group with substantial resources of one sort or another, and you could name a beneficiary of the Pentagon.

A Received Value Mix: 1961

When John F. Kennedy took the oath of office in January of 1961, he inherited a peacetime military force that was more powerful than any on earth. He was also the recipient of a set of values which I rather loosely typify as *pax americana*. The presidency since Roosevelt's day had become the key actor in the realm, and as Kennedy took office, it was clear that he planned to be his own secretary of state. The maintenance of world peace through American military power depended not upon diplomats, but upon warriors.[10]

The received value of a *pax americana*, based essentially on the idea of nuclear deterrence, was not without its critics. People argued over

[9] RAND is the archetype of what Don K. Price was talking about in *Government and Science* (New York: New York University Press, 1954), Chapter 3, "Federalism by Contract." For a history and descriptive analysis of RAND, see Bruce L. R. Smith, *The RAND Corporation* (Cambridge: Harvard University Press, 1966).

[10] This view is most clearly reflected in the memoirs of Kennedy's "favorite soldier." In *Swords and Plowshares* (New York: Norton, 1972), p. 419, General Maxwell D. Taylor writes:

> The members of our diplomatic service perform well their traditional representational functions abroad, observing and reporting the world scene to Washington in well-written appreciations. But such functions, important as they are, do not require and rarely develop officials of the take-charge type capable of holding their own against tough-minded, well-trained adversaries. By temperament and training our diplomats are rarely experienced executives and it is probably unfair to expect them to change.

theories of "containment," "tripwires," "protracted conflict,"[11] and the need for response capabilities short of the holocaust. The notion of America as policeman of the world was not, however, subject to much debate or discussion. Indeed, like all received values, it had become part of the conventional wisdom of the time and had been enshrined in all manner of formal structures and in the "hearts and minds" of the public and the "best and brightest" as well.

Civilian control was another matter completely. The role of the military and more specifically, the professional military, in a democratic society had been a problem for generations. Simply put, it was the problem of power coupled with expertise. How does one make choices from among alternatives proffered by lifetime professionals who have an axe to grind? The dilemma took on special significance by 1961 because so much of foreign policy and domestic politico-economic life was wrapped up in the answer(s). Harold Lasswell's "Garrison State" argument, made in 1937, had proved to be chillingly correct:[12] The world had become dominated by the managers of extreme coercion, and the age of diplomacy rooted in economic interest was waning.

Lasswell was also correct in his belief that increasing the variety and supply of new weapons had not reduced nations' propensity to conflict. Indeed, the reverse seemed true. When people saw the first barrage balloons and the bombing of civilian targets in World War I, many believed that mankind would be forced to come to its senses and create a world order, lest it be destroyed by the devastating aggressiveness of nation states. By 1961, however, the world was dominated by super-powers capable of destroying the planet, and wars of varying size had dominated the period since Lasswell made his prophetic remarks.[13]

The problem of civilian control had taken on this new and frightening dimension. The absolute control of the military by political leaders was, if anything, a more imperative received value than it had been twenty years before. Kennedy managed to make certain that he retained control over the capacity to order nuclear retaliation. He had no reason to

---

[11] The containment theory was first voiced by George F. Kennan in "The Sources of Soviet Conduct," *Foreign Affairs* (July, 1947), p. 210; tripwire theory must be attributed to Herman Kahn, *On Escalation* (New York: Praeger, 1965). In his *Protracted Conflict*, Robert Strausz-Hupe traces the origin of this term to Mao Tse-tung, *On the Protracted War* (Peking: Foreign Languages Press, 1960).

[12] The argument is first stated in "Sino–Japanese Crisis: The Garrison State Versus the Civilian State," *China Quarterly*, XI (1937), 643–649.

[13] Lasswell reiterates this point in Samuel P. Huntington, *Changing Patterns of Military Politics* (New York: Free Press, 1962).

fear a coup, but he understood very clearly that in crisis situations he personally would have to insure that standing orders did not provoke military situations that would leave him without alternatives.[14] The problem of the political power of the military–industrial–university complex was not so straightforward.

Kennedy was faced with a realm of national defense that had developed its own political strength. That which Eisenhower had helped to create had gotten completely out of direct control. To fight or not to fight remained a presidential decision to be shared with Congress (although Congress seemed to have lost some of the effective power to declare war by acquiescing to the argument that instant response would be required given the rapidity of possible nuclear attack). The question of which weapons to build for what kinds of potential conflicts lay in military hands in 1961. The DOD and its friends in Congress and in the political system had effectively determined the drift of weapons development, procurement, and strategic choices. It was this aspect of civilian control that had been lost and that Kennedy and his cohorts wished to regain. The received value of civilian control was as contradictory as always, but the basic contradictions were compounded not only by the vastness and ramifications of the military enterprise but also by the presence of large numbers of civilian actors whose interests were ineluctably mixed with those of the military because science and technology had become weapons.

Science and technology as weapons conjures visions of people in white coats surrounded by esoteric machines. This is somewhat misleading in the context of the national defense realm. The idea for a weapon system and its transformation into a prototype capable of industrial fabrication necessarily involves the elaborate coordination of a large and complex variety of skills and people. DOD and its constituent and client organizations had developed elaborate man–machine systems which were, according to many critics, uncoordinated and inefficient. The decision to develop a weapon system under the Eisenhower administration was at best a haphazard event unrelated to any grand design. Each service tended to develop its own constituency and clientele networks. The fusion of civilian scientists, engineers, and managers inside and outside the Pentagon made it difficult, if not impossible, to find out what was in progress and why.

---

[14] See Graham T. Allison, *Essence of Decision* (Boston: Little, Brown, 1971) and Robert F. Kennedy, *Thirteen Days* (New York: Norton, 1969).

Critics and supporters of defense policy became actual or potential resources of one sort or another in the realm of national defense. By 1961 military policy questions were defined increasingly in the esoterica of science and technology.[15] The lesson of the twenty years prior to Kennedy's inauguration was that such people were the key elements in the race with the Russians for a position of superiority. The ideas that could generate new weapons were in large part discoverable outside the military services. The means for their achievement and the analysis of their probable effects and costs were essentially in the cooperative systems developed by military and civilian managers and engineers.

By 1961 some unanticipated negative consequences of weapons development programs begun years before were becoming apparent. Scientific and technological realms attached to the different military services were spending and committing billions of dollars to programs that too often produced obsolete, ineffective, or inappropriate weapons. This was not because of any great lack on the part of research and development (R&D) people. They were not, after all, in the business of defining the goals or priorities in weapons development. They were specialists and professionals of the highest order and worked at the behest of others. Once an initial appropriation was made, the costs of weapons systems seemed nearly uncontrollable over time. Kennedy was determined to gain a measure of control over the weapons procurement process while expanding its significance in the output mix of the federal government.

The Apotheosis of Rationality and the Garrison State: 1961–1976

The TFX and the Politics of Bureaucracy

The focus of the analysis narrows to a consideration of an instance of weapons procurement. TFX (Tactical Fighter Experimental) illustrates a number of significant phenomena salient to the realm and to the future of politics as well. These are:

[15] Morris Janowitz, *The Professional Soldier* (New York: Free Press, 1960). Janowitz suggested that the military of 1960 ". . . seems to have been almost converted into a giant engineering establishment," p. 21.

1. The apotheosis of rationality in decision making as a received value.
2. An attempt at intrarealm political change through managerial power clothed in newly professionalized expertise.
3. The conflict and cooperation patterns of entrenched professionalized bureaucrats faced with an intrarealm challenge.
4. An effort to solve a problem and to plan, predict, and manage complex interdependent and interactive systems.

The easiest way to proceed is with an institutional description of top-level DOD personnel in terms of their routes of entry and formal chain of command. Fox provides such a description for DOD in the early 1970s:[16]

More than two million people are employed by the Department of Defense. It is the largest single-unit bureaucracy in the world. The men and women who govern this bureaucracy and are responsible for the nation's defense capabilities are divided among three categories: (1) civilians nominated by the President and approved by the Senate; (2) senior career military officers (Army and Air Force generals and Navy admirals); and (3) senior career civil service personnel.

The Secretary of Defense, a civilian appointee, is the highest ranking official in the Department. The Secretary's immediate staff consists of fifteen civilians, nominated by the President with the Secretary's counsel: two Deputy Secretaries of Defense, the Director of Defense Research and Engineering, eight Assistant Secretaries of Defense, and four Assistants to the Secretary.

The President also appoints Secretaries of the Army, the Navy, and the Air Force. Each service Secretary reports directly to the Secretary of Defense. Each has a chief assistant, called the Undersecretary of the Army, Navy, or Air Force, and four Assistant Secretaries. Each of the Assistant Secretaries directs one of the following areas within his service: (1) financial management; (2) installations and logistics; (3) manpower and reserve affairs; (4) research and development. These five civilian officials are nominated by the President with the advice of the Secretary of Defense. Each service Secretary has a staff of several hundred military and civilian personnel.

Also reporting to the civilian Secretary of each service is the military Chief of Staff of the service. Each Chief of Staff is appointed by the President and becomes the senior military officer in his branch of the armed services. The President also appoints a Chairman of the Joint Chiefs of Staff from one of the services. The individual Chiefs of Staff are directly responsible to the Secretary of Defense as well as to the Secretaries of their respective services. The Chairman of the Joint Chiefs of Staff reports to the Secretary of Defense. The Office of the Joint Chiefs of Staff employs approximately 2,000 military and civilian personnel. In addition, each Chief of Staff is served by several thousand military and civilian personnel. A military officer working for a Chief of Staff also serves the Secretary of his service. Although the Secretary is the senior official within the Pentagon, officers receive their military promotions on the basis of evaluations from their military superiors, including their Chiefs of Staff. This fact is especially significant during periods of controversy between Secretaries or Assistant Secretaries of a service and the Chief of Staff.

Most senior defense officials and their staffs—about 26,000 people in all—work in the Pentagon. The division of civilian and military personnel within the Pentagon is about even.

The domains represented by the three services, presidential appointees, and permanent civil servants plus their constituency and clientele networks in Congress, the media, and private sector economic concerns are the core of the general realm. The opportunities for conflict and cooperation between these crosscutting specific realms are substantial, and the problems of communication, planning, environmental change, and personnel turnover compound them. Fox points out that the average incumbency of assistant secretaries has been about three years, which is also the approximate tour of Pentagon duty for most senior officers.

When President Kennedy appointed Robert S. McNamara as secretary of defense, he set in motion one of the most significant political battles in the history of American public bureaucracy. What I shall call "the McNamara group" entered the appointive positions with reasonably full knowledge of the problems posed by the sheer size and complexity of the Department. They were among the most knowledgeable outsiders ever to try to take over a government agency. The term *take over* is not hyperbolic. Kennedy and McNamara understood DOD and its domination by the military and its constituency and clientele networks. The problem was to gain control of the crucial decision structures involving procurement, research and development, and long-range planning.

The *modus operandi* for this assault on bureaucratic power was provided by new "defense intellectuals." During the 1950s a series of books critical of the goals of strategic doctrine and of the ways of maximizing their attainment appeared. The RAND Corporation provided the ideas and the men to bring these criticisms to alter the existing procedures of the DOD. A landmark book in 1960 entitled *The Economics of Defense in the Nuclear Age* attempted to demonstrate that a whole new way of looking at and organizing the realm of national defense was in order.[17] Hitch, a former Yale economics professor, became the comptroller of DOD under McNamara. The thrust of the book and of much that followed in DOD was that the techniques of rational economic analysis should (and could) be applied to the structure and function of the DOD. Much of the thinking of Hitch and McKean became institutionalized in the form of a Programming, Planning, Budgeting System (PPBS) and systems analysis, an office of which was established in the Office of the Secretary.

Without going into elaborate detail, the idea was to create a system based on formal rules and quantifiable utilities that would permit informed and rational choice between missions, tactics, and weapons systems in service of a general plan. One of the first things McNamara did was to establish an annually revised Five-Year Defense Force Structure Plan, later modified to the Five-Year Defense Plan. The Plan was a structured, compulsory routine, designed to cut unilateral weapons acquisition moves and to coordinate the services procurement schemes directly with national security objectives.

Two kinds of connections were involved. National security objectives were to determine weapons system development. The idea of a balance of nuclear terror had been roundly criticized as being ineffective in the face of provocations short of superpower collisions. The argument was made most persuasively by a professor of political science named Henry A. Kissinger. In *Nuclear Weapons and Foreign Policy*, published in 1957,[18] he argued that in a nuclear stalemate, subversion, wars of national liberation, and guerrilla wars could nip away incrementally at the nonaligned or "free world" nations while America was prepared only for massive deterrence. An alteration of strategic planning to deal with "brushfire" wars would logically involve some heavy losses on the part of those whose careers, fortunes, and factories were dedicated to massive retaliation and the technology that supported it. This "new connection" between national defense planning and weapons procurement posed an

---

[17] Charles J. Hitch and Roland N. McKean, *The Economics of Defense in the Nuclear Age* (Cambridge, Mass.: Harvard University Press, 1963).
[18] Kissinger, *Nuclear Weapons and Foreign Policy.*

immediate threat to the structures of stability created around the defense posture of the Eisenhower years.

A second connection relative to the actions of the McNamara group involved the general issue of duplication and commonality. As suggested above, the services had traditionally procured what they needed independently of one another. From shoelaces to aircraft, the services went their separate ways. This state of affairs violated all the instincts of the systems analysts, economists, and managers like McNamara. It was wasteful, it took no account of possible economies of scale, and it resulted in substantial duplication. To remove the services one step from their procurement and R&D structures, however, was to threaten formidable configurations of intrarealm power.

The battle between the McNamara group, the military services, and their allies in the realm was joined in a number of arenas. In many ways, the R&D/procurement conflicts best illustrate the McNamara effort and its opposition. The most famous of these conflicts was the TFX controversy. TFX represented the Air Force's dream of a tactical interceptor aircraft for the 1970s and 1980s. By virtue of a swing-wing design, the aircraft was to be capable of supersonic as well as extraordinarily slow low-level flight. The operational aircraft was named F-111.

The TFX story illustrates the variety of realms involved in the national defense realm. It also tells much about the attempt by the president and his appointees to seize crucial decision-making power in weapons procurement under the guise of a managerial ideology. McNamara, Hitch, and company argued for cost-effective defense wherever possible. This notion was understood to be a strategic problem as well as a managerial ideology. At the macroscopic level, models (or scenarios) of possible combat situations were projected to devise best-fit strategies for multiple and varied responses. Analysis of possible contingencies and possible responses could be done by using economic and rational actor modeling techniques. Computers capable of storing data and programs beyond man's memory could, by the early 1960s, be used to plug in limitless combinations of values to simulate changes in the hypothetical world of strategy making. The politics of strategists, then, was one front for conflict between the McNamara group and the Joint Chiefs, certain congressmen and senators, and the long-time senior civil servants of the Pentagon.

The second front involved the microscopic employment of similar techniques; although the managerial assault on the old structures of power differed in significant ways, it still rested on rational actor calculations. Designing an aircraft of great complexity, many of whose components constitute state-of-the-art technology and beyond, is a *creative* process involving the labors of thousands of highly skilled people. Like war, the next airplane will probably look pretty much like the last one. It will be in large measure a product of custom and convention in design and production. Innovations tend to be elaborations or extensions of the past. But this process does not occur in an ivory tower: In this realm it is closely tied to one's estimate of a distant future in which the weapon under consideration must *outperform* the enemy's weapon if it is to have utility. It must also be reliable and affordable. *Affordable* is used with the greatest temerity, for although it is and always has been a standard incantation of defense planners and others, I am convinced of the melancholy observation of the late Senator Richard Russell, chairman of the Senate Armed Services Committee, who said, "There is something about preparing for destruction that causes men to be more careless in spending money than they would be if they were building for constructive purposes."[19]

In the case of TFX, McNamara was prepared to link up the values of high-technology weapons development with strategic modeling and the managerial ideology of cost effectiveness under norms of mission-centered rationality. In other words, instead of simply asking "what will this aircraft do?" PPBS ideology would question the kinds of tactical missions that could be fulfilled; TFX would be looked at as a component of a *weapons mix* to be employed in some future military conflict. No more disjointed, uncoordinated weapons procurement would be tolerated. From design to deployment, TFX was to be part of a series of *systemic* phenomena such that one would know its role, its cost (absolutely and in terms of trade-offs), and its function within the mix of weapons systems deployed to meet a finite number of hostility probabilities. TFX was perfect for the assault on traditional, mindless incrementalism in the procurement process.

TFX was conceived as an Air Force tactical interceptor by General F. F. Everest who assumed command of the Tactical Air Command in 1959. According to Robert J. Art[20] (upon whose excellent narrative much of this discussion is based), Everest paid lip service to the traditional

---

[19] Fox, *Arming America*, p. 151.
[20] Robert J. Art, *The TFX Decision: McNamara and the Military* (Boston: Little, Brown, 1968).

fighter mission of air-to-air combat, close-in ground support of combat troops and supply interdiction capabilities. Art believes that Everest, operating under the massive retaliation norms of the Eisenhower years, wanted TFX mainly for its designed capacity to make low-level supersonic dashes under radar for purposes of dropping nuclear payloads. Certainly his thought included the traditional TAC (Tactical Air Command) mission, but the aircraft was also to be designed to carry out the latter mission as well. In any event, by 1960 work at NASA confirmed the feasibility of the swing-wing concept.

The Air Research and Development Command and the Tactical Air Command presented the Director of R&D a Specific Operational Requirement detailing the needs and performance requirements of a new tactical interceptor aircraft for TAC. The Director of R&D, who reports directly to the Secretary, was supposed to make a source selection for R&D, the next step in the usual procedure, but he decided to hold up the process at this point (October, 1960). The setting for the first major intrarealm confrontation was established.

In February of 1961 the Secretary shocked the realm by announcing that TFX would be made to fulfill the requirements of the Army, Navy, and the Air Force. In the late spring of that year he changed his mind and announced that only the Navy and Air Force would have TFX in common. "Commonality" came into the language as McNamara used TFX to propound his views that independent procurement fiefdoms could endure only if they met cost-effective and mission-appropriate criteria.

The Navy and Air Force responded to McNamara by saying that despite consultation, they could not reach agreement over joint requirements for TFX. McNamara replied by unilaterally issuing his own set of requirements. The pitch of the battle intensified as the aggrieved generals and admirals began to quietly explain the depths of McNamara's heresy to friends in Congress and in the press. A civilian with no experience in these matters had not only rejected their proposals but had countermanded them. The civil–military problem at this point became a civil–military–technological–managerial problem. The cutting edge of a new kind of politics involving actors removed from the electoral process was beginning to take shape. The ancient conflict over scarce public resources lay beneath it, but in TFX a most dramatic example of the new politics of complexity management under rationality norms could be seen.

Following the commonality order, the Air Force issued a request for proposals for McNamara's TFX. The major airframe companies submitted proposals to an Air Force Source Selection Board (one is created for each major weapons system) within a few months of the request. There are traditional clients who have over the years been the recipients of airframe contracts from the Navy and the Air Force. Grumman has been building naval aircraft for generations (between 1965 and 1969 anywhere from 31% to 55% of that company's business was done with DOD). The major airframe contractor for the Air Force was Boeing, which does about one-third of its business with DOD. In order to compete with Boeing's superior resources, Grumman temporarily combined with General Dynamics of Houston, Texas, in an attempt to win the TFX contract.

The Source Selection Board chose Boeing unanimously. The Air Force Council (a higher body) overturned the decision and ordered an extension of competition between Cencral Dynamics/Grumman and Boeing. The Board again chose Boeing, but this time around the Navy refused to go along, arguing that its special needs (aircraft carrier features) were not met by the Boeing design. The respective service secretaries reversed the choice of the Board once again and ordered yet another round of competition. During these intervals the companies were revising cost and performance estimates to the point where any reasonable observer might have questioned the eventual price tag and performance features.

The identical sequence of choosing Boeing and having the choice rejected by the Navy and the civilian appointees was repeated once again! Finally, McNamara ordered a terminal run off, altering the contract specifications to include "payoff points" for commonality. A fourth and final set of proposals was submitted by the companies to the Source Selection Board, which once again found in favor of Boeing. McNamara and the civilian appointees then announced their decision to award the contract to General Dynamics/Grumman. A Senate investigation headed by Senator McClellan began faster than you can say TFX. Senator Jackson, Kennedy's campaign manager, was terribly concerned, since Boeing was a crucial industrial employer in his state of Washington. Vice President Lyndon B. Johnson and Secretary of the Navy John Connally were pleased that General Dynamics was among the favored.

The story goes on and on and can be found in Senate testimony[21]

[21] U.S., Congress, Senate. Permanent Subcommittee on Investigations of the Senate Committee on Government Operations. *Hearings on the TFX Contract Investigation*, 10 volumes (Washington, D.C.: U.S. Government Printing Office, 1963–1964).

and in the popular press. Briefly, General Dynamics/Grumman was not able to build the airplane without substantial subcontracting to Boeing.

By the time F-111 was born, there were two versions, Navy and Air Force. When the aircraft became operational and was tested in field conditions in Viet Nam (about five years after the final award), it suffered from a variety of ills that caused it to crash with alarming frequency. The cost of the delivered aircraft was well beyond the initial estimates.[22] The final cost of the F-111 program was approximately $11 million per aircraft. The Navy refused to order any of the planes and proceeded to develop the F-14 as its principal tactical aircraft.

This narrative provides some of the major themes discoverable in the politics of this realm and illuminates some interesting patterns of conflict and cooperation within the setting of high-technology development management and resource allocation. The F-111 was one of a genre: extremely expensive weapons systems constructed almost like one-of-a-kind buildings or monuments. Technologies of different sorts must be amassed over a long period of time for design and development. Tens of thousands of drawings, tests, and estimates must be made before even a mockup of a plane can be built. Millions of dollars must be bet against the ability of engineers and managers to solve problems as they arise.

The TFX vignette illustrates some of the factors that I believe to be of great significance not only to this realm but to others as well. I have discussed the power and prestige of professionalism in the context of all three realms. But in no realm is it more significant than this one, for it is in the national defense area that nearly every significant actor has claim to some profession or other. To repeat, the significance of profession lies not only in its capacity to dominate thought and action in its domain; the concept is also of vital political importance in that it identifies a population of actors whose interests involve the struggles over allocation of scarce public resources in part defined by the language of profession. In TFX, McNamara fought the entrenched professionals to a draw *by introducing a loosely defined professional domain as a contender for dominance of the realm.*

The new profession, of course, was not all that new. It was characterized by the application of a series of ideas derived from the study of management and economic analysis. These ideas became identified with

[22] John Steinbruner and Barry Carter, "Organizational and Political Dimensions of the Strategic Posture: The Problems of Reform," *Daedalus* (Summer, 1975), p. 131.

and systematized by the McNamara group. Thus, the managerial profession/systems analysis civilians represented a set of ideas and were themselves powerful hierarchical actors by virtue of McNamara's support and the resources which he placed at their disposal.

PPBS, Program Evaluation and Review Technique (PERT), and Managing by Objective (MBO) are not panaceas for solving the major problem of complex technological interdependence management.[23] At best, they constitute informative and occasionally useful means of illuminating costs and interdependencies. At worst, their vocabularies, mathematical formulations, and vague generalizations serve as a powerful, professionalized mask, implying quantified truth when little exists. The complexity revealed by McNamara's insistence on cost-benefit analysis and his use of the system metaphor are significant for our purposes in part because they beg the questions of value and theory without which "facts" are useless.

Consider TFX and the question of benefit. Certainly one can see that the abstract notion of *commonality* when concretely applied to weapons systems is a good idea. It is good if it husbands scarce resources. Spare parts, technical drawings and manuals, technician training programs, and the like are cheaper to create and maintain for one airplane than for two.

A second benefit arises from aggregating functions within one weapons system. As originally conceived the TFX would have been capable of everything—strategic nuclear attack from land or sea, low-level ground support, and supersonic dogfighting. The value maximized by such a dream is *flexibility*. This becomes even more significant when coupled with a third benefit that would presumably follow from constructing a weapons system in this manner.

This third benefit accrues to the nation when TFX is capable of being integrated into *long-range strategic planning*. Certainly its role as conceived in 1961 could be seen in nearly every strategic contingency imaginable to the wargamesmen in the Pentagon. If Kissinger and others were correct in their predictions that under a doctrine of massive retaliation America could be nibbled to death by provocations less than nuclear, then here indeed was a weapon system for all seasons.

---

[23] For a critical review of the budgetary significance of the McNamara revolution, see Leonard Merewitz and Stephen Sosnick, *The Budget's New Clothes* (Chicago: Markham, 1971) and Aaron Wildavsky, *The Politics of the Budgetary Process*, 2nd ed. (Boston: Little, Brown, 1964).

Finally, TFX can be understood as a symbol of the newly formalized multiple contingency planning going on in the Pentagon. Depending upon the nature, duration, and location of conflict, a series of flexibly designed systems were to be capable of rapid deployment. The central message of the new ideology was that *given a carefully stipulated goal, rational analysis could provide the most effective solution for the least cost.*

In order for this state of grace to come into being, the realm of national defense had to be organized to maximize the possibility of the desired outcome. The McNamara group wanted to reintroduce market and market-like constraints, compel compliance with performance standards, and eliminate cost overruns that were not a result of contract modification. The battle was against a host of entrenched actors within the realm. The parochialism of the services had led to disjointed and wasteful weapons systems. Congress was populated by too many beneficiaries of the antiquated incrementalism that kept unnecessary and costly operations going in order to maintain good constituency relations. Permanent civil servants had grown powerful in service to the old incrementalist management routines. All the significant actors in the weapons procurement process had become uncomfortably friendly and tolerant toward defense contractors.

The McNamara intrusion into the ordinary procedures of the realm stemmed from that important, modern mixture of political power and professionalized rationality. It was directed at genuine problems, but perhaps too much was expected of it. The ideology of rational management in service of mission, function, or objective in the realm of national defense suffers from serious flaws which are worth discussing, because the politics of this realm are likely to be significant indicators of the role of bureaucracy in the future of American political life. The McNamara group and its thought can be understood and criticized in a number of ways using TFX as an example. One can conceive of it as a way of thinking about national policy formation, as a way of organizing powerful political actors into structures of action and control, and as a means of policy evaluation.

One has little to quibble about with *any systematic* way of thinking about national policy formation, since precious little of it goes on. The McNamara group, through systems analysis, sought to probe the interrelatedness of programs and their varied impacts *before* they occurred. Simply put, McNamara and company introduced the first serious attempt at comprehensive interactive planning of all defense inputs and outputs in the history of the armed forces. The very notion of such planning implied a threat to the *status quo ante* of the professionalized military because of the massive centralization of decision making about scarce resources. It also involved a series of means–ends statements that can become intertwined in some unfortunate ways. If one can refine measurement of inputs (equipment, personnel, supplies, facilities, and funds) and outputs (the B-52 force, the Polaris force, etc.), then the problem is in one sense close to solution. But the problem of means–ends statements is also one of teleology. Each means becomes an end, and each end becomes a means. Thus, the question must arise as to the true output nature of Polaris, for instance.

A weapons system is at best a *proximate* output whose ultimate purpose must be understood not only in terms of cost effectiveness or multiple strategy roles but in terms of some other values as well. One simply cannot leap from dollar costs per effective megatonnage delivered (or some other efficiency criterion) to statements about the ultimate purpose of the weapon. Polaris and its ilk are conceived and multiply under received values which by definition are seldom challenged and which alter slowly through time. Thus, the Soviet (and to a lesser extent, the Chinese) threat is understood to be a constant, as are the inflationary and salubrious effects of defense spending on the nation's economy. At the crucial level of national policy, the techniques of rational decision making cannot tell us what *ought* to happen or what we *ought* to do, because these techniques cannot deal with that which is not quantifiable.[24]

In a sense such criticism is unfair, because the techniques themselves do not fail or misrepresent; the people who employ them do. The McNamara "revolution" could be fully effective only if DOD knew how much was "enough" defense and understood the ultimate ends of its mission in terms appropriate to its methodology. "Keeping all Americans safe" is a reassuring end-statement, but it hardly qualifies as the other side of the efficiency/effectiveness equation.

[24] The problem of the relationship between facts and values, means and ends in decision making precedes the McNamara era, of course. Significant statements of the problem can be found in Chester I. Barnard, *The Functions of the Executive* (Cambridge, Mass.: Harvard University Press, 1938); Herbert A. Simon, *Administrative Behavior* (New York: Free Press, 1945) and *The Sciences of the Artificial* (Cambridge, Mass.: M.I.T. Press, 1969); and David Braybrooke and Charles E. Lindblom, *A Strategy of Decision* (New York: Free Press, 1963).

In attempting to win their battle with the entrenched forces of the national defense realm, the McNamara group and defense intellectuals in general tended to let their enthusiasm outrun their methodology. What began as a series of management techniques became something more in the heat of intrarealm conflict. Without attempting to affix blame and without elaborate analysis, it is clear that the techniques of managing weapons procurement and the deployment of systems did affect the conduct of the Viet Nam War.

It must be recalled that the bright young men of the Kennedy–Johnson years were responsible not only for an assault on the national defense realm. They were also effective competitors in the realm of foreign affairs. Imbued with a way of looking at one sort of organizational reality and seeing parts of their realm involved, the McNamara group (which included some high-ranking military men like General Taylor) soon found themselves quantifying the war in Viet Nam. Claims were made that rested on quantification and rational analysis. "Light at the end of the tunnel," "Vietnamization," and "body counts" recall the sad results of attempting to apply a specific kind of organizational analysis to an inappropriate environment.

David Halberstam identifies this as the simple hubris of the "best and the brightest"[25] men of their generation being led astray by the special snobbery of intellectuals in combat with bureaucrats both in and out of uniform. There is much truth to this claim, but I wonder how many other professionals might be tempted to take their beliefs into new situations incrementally, almost mindlessly, in the honest faith that the techniques of their existence have utility in seemingly related situations.

More than any other war in American history Viet Nam was an organizational event. It proceeded from and fed upon information distortion. In part this came from hierarchical and functional mischief caused by competition between intelligence services and from outright lies by high officials. It also stemmed from the common phenomena contributing to distortion in feedback loops of any large size.[26] Alteration of information occurs as a result of faulty encoding/decoding and/or the desire to make the situation appear favorable in terms of one's prior claims.

[25] David Halberstam, *The Best and the Brightest* (New York: Random House, 1969).

[26] *Cf.* Karl W. Deutsch, *The Nerves of Government* (New York: Free Press, 1966). For an interesting contrast between the rational decision-making model and a cybernetic formulation in defense planning, see John D. Steinbruner, *The Cybernetic Theory of Decision* (Princeton: Princeton University Press, 1974).

Finally, despite the best efforts of McNamara and others, the war was the quintessence of disjointed incrementalism. Rather than being effectively planned in a comprehensive manner as McNamara had wanted, it came close to the classic incrementalist pattern of pouring more water on the fire without ever looking closely at the nature of the fire itself.

My point is that the techniques of the McNamara revolution have nothing to do with the received values that got us into the Viet Nam War and will get us into the next war. Program budgeting, planning, managing by objective, and systems analysis cannot deal with the ultimate end-states toward which policy is directed. This bundle of techniques should not be used as a basis for such value claims, nor should they be dismissed for their failure to be a substitute for politics itself. The techniques of management introduced by McNamara do have utility and applicability within this realm and elsewhere. They have been and will continue to be vital elements in the language and thought of politics.

If I may be permitted the coinage of yet another dreadful acronym, I would like to group together a set of techniques used to maximize rational decision making in the realm of national defense. Management of Complex Technological Interdependencies (MOCTI) summarizes all planning, budgeting, forecasting, and evaluational techniques used to promote rational (i.e., intended, cost-effective, proximate) end-states. MOCTI also suggests structural alterations in conformance with its core value of rationality. As a set of valuative procedures, MOCTI alters organizational structures by demanding information which is either new or in different formats, and thus requires new analytical and professionalized skills. As a conceptual scheme, vocabulary, and organizational structure, MOCTI suggests conflict between its values of centralized coordination of information and values held by institutionalized professionals, clients, and constituents of the realm. The key to the growing power of MOCTI lies in its control over information flows and its ability to apply its values to those of its intrarealm competitors. As it comes to dominate the language of analysis, it will come to have greater control over the structural artifacts of authority.

The information that MOCTI creates and controls has great significance beyond the realm of national defense. This collection of techniques and the actors associated with them lost much ground when President Johnson attempted to diffuse them throughout the administrative structures of the federal government. The manuals and structural rearrangements implied by PPBS had proved either inappropriate, too disruptive of the existing configurations of power and inertia, or incomprehensible to those charged with the responsibility for implementation. Although the MOCTI ideas and the people identified with them may have passed from the limelight, the problems with which they were to deal persist.

It should be clear from the discussion thus far that no single person or group of persons knows all of what the realm of national defense may be doing at any given moment. Scale and complexity explain the impossibility of *knowing* this in any conventional sense. These two factors do not, however, preclude knowledge: They simply demand that things be known in a different way. In general, we do know the linear effects of weapons procurement: We comprehend that after a period of eight years or so some branch of the armed forces will possess a weapons system of effectiveness X at cost Y with benefit Z. We also have some knowledge of nonlinear events associated with the research, development, engineering, production, and maintenance of the system, particularly in terms of their effects on domestic economic variables. And we have some idea of the labor, capital, and inflationary effects of the project. MOCTI provides an initial step toward understanding the gross interactive impact of a weapon on systems inside and outside the realm of national defense.

As interactive and interdependent proximate and long-range implications of policy choice become more apparent, understanding for purposes of control becomes more imperative. Recent warnings of interactive technological doom have come from a variety of sources, all of which have a central, often unspoken, premise: that the world, however defined, is a system (or has systemic properties).[27] MOCTI is the study of interactive technological systems narrowly focused in the realm of national defense. It is an irony for the future of politics that this realm should be one of the places where people are being trained to think about this sort of interdependence. I hesitate to conclude that they are in fact managing it, but it is within this realm that embryonic attempts are being made.[28] No method has yet been found to insure performance standards or to prevent cost overruns.

Despite this unfortunate situation, there are few places other than

[27] See Jacques Ellul, *The Technological Society* (New York: Vintage, 1964) and Robert L. Heilbroner, *An Inquiry into the Human Prospect* (New York: Norton, 1975).

[28] A fascinating, if highly technical, review of these attempts is contained in Joseph P. Martino, *Technological Forecasting for Decision Making* (New York: American Elsevier, 1972) and an outstanding description of management success can be found in Harvey M. Sapolsky, *The Polaris System Development* (Cambridge, Mass.: Harvard University Press, 1972). Sapolsky illustrates the political character of PERT as a protective device for the Navy's Special Projects Office.

within the MOCTI experience where one can look for the combination of management and analysis of complex technological interdependence. The organizational skills needed to put together high-technology weapons systems and to assess their impact are, I think, the precursors of an age when politics and administration are likely to become even more inextricably linked than they are today.

Under any circumstances, MOCTI cannot go beyond the teleological trap unless its adherents become the most powerful actors in all realms and enjoy widespread support among constituencies. If that day should come and if MOCTI should become part of the received value mix of the entire political order, then even the refocused concepts of political power offered in this book would be woefully outdated and inappropriate.

Constituents, Clients, and Victims in the Garrison State

The defeat in Viet Nam left the *pax americana* of the last thirty years in questionable condition. Perhaps it is no longer true that America should be the policeman of the world, fighting communist aggression wherever it appears or seems to appear. But a large-scale push is apparently underway to reequip the armed forces, and the idea of *pax americana* is dependent upon the existence of large military forces and high-technology weapons capable of rapid deployment. The development of new generations of post–Viet Nam weaponry implies the high probability of their use. The common-sense notion that the presence of a weapon all but guarantees its use is not refuted by the fact that since Hiroshima and Nagasaki no one has used nuclear weapons. The failure to use nuclear weapons tells us something about their utility: They are valuable only as an ultimate and desperate threat.

New bombers, cruise missiles, supertanks, and assorted rocketry ordnance can be used as their predecessors were. No matter what our public foreign policy statements may be, our pattern of defense spending and that of the U.S.S.R. suggests that the two premier superpowers will continue to develop the capacity to go to war any place on the globe. The cold war rested on superiority and then on parity in variegated destructive power. Whatever we call it today rests on the same assumption, without, perhaps, the 1950–1970 naiveté that military might alone could guarantee worldwide conformance to American desires.

The structures, customs, and belief systems of the realm of national defense remain wrapped up in the received value which I call *pax americana*. It is a value which may be as internally contradictory and as subject to lag as any value discussed so far. The changes in the world environment, the need to increase our effective capability to destroy our enemies with weapons neither side believes it can use, and our demonstrated inability through military power or foreign aid to compel significant changes in the political systems of some relatively powerless nations are contradictory to the logic of *pax americana*. Despite the contradictory possibilities inherent in the value, however, major change has not come to pass.

In part this can be explained in terms of the vested interests of some of the major realms within the general realm of national defense. I have discussed the career military and noted that its existence is partially predicated on the expansion of technology and the increased opportunity for command inherent in near-war and wartime conditions. A similar pattern of interest is discoverable in the permanent civilian structures within the realm. Constituents of the realm, including powerful congressmen and senators, have built careers around a strong national defense. The client contractors (those whose total business is at least one-third dependent upon defense contracts) and the constituent contractors (those who do less than one-third of their business with DOD) further reinforce the *pax americana* value.[29]

As potent as all of these structures are, they still rest on a widely accepted received value that holds international communism to be a constant danger that can be countered only by heavy defense expenditures. This permanent condition of near-war frightened Harold Lasswell thirty-five years ago when he coined the term *garrison state*. The *garrison state* is one in which the military is a permanent and pervasive entity whose existence is discoverable in nearly every facet of organized life.

The military has become a fixture in peacetime America in a variety of ways during the last thirty-five years. Patriotism and military heroics are fused in popular culture. The vast expansion of the military presence into a permanent social and economic fixture of everyday America has

[29] This is my arbitrary division, based partially on the data in Fox's *Arming America* and Melman's *Pentagon Capitalism: The Political Economy of War* (New York: McGraw-Hill, 1970).

great import for many reasons, not the least of which is its common acceptance as a natural part of the social order. There were few who doubted the sense and propriety of this permanent military presence until the Viet Nam War which, among other things, caused some questions to be raised about the nature of citizenship in the garrison state.

Traditionally, citizenship in any nation has entailed the obligation for military service in time of national emergency. From Lincoln's time through Korea, conscription never enjoyed much popularity in America. The notions of participatory government and conscription were probably always contradictory. The contradiction in most instances was resolved by patriotism inflamed by righteous indignation over enemy behavior. Of course, the basic coercive power of the state had to be used on the occasionally irresolute, the draft evader, or the conscientious objector.

The Viet Nam War placed the newly expanded peacetime military squarely in the midst of the conditions of citizenship outlined in this book. The war required that people be drafted. The deferment pattern of the 1950s had insured that those who were in college or engaged in agriculture or in a defense industry could avoid service. Volunteers before Viet Nam were most likely to be low on the socio-economic ladder of American life. When the War heated up, people began to notice the disproportionate numbers of minority and poor combat soldiers who were drafted and sent to Viet Nam. Deferments were disallowed as new troops were needed, and draft boards managed to conscript those who did not have the dollars, knowledge, or lawyers to circumvent the draft laws.

White, middle-class college students suddenly discovered that they had to actively combat the bureaucratic agents of the state in order to avoid the draft. Most of them managed to avoid it, because they had one or more of the needed resources mentioned above. But how might one typify those citizens who lacked those resources? The poor, the ignorant, and the resourceless were *victimized*. The inequities of the draft highlighted not only the inequalities of the American population, but also the differential treatment offered by a supposedly even-handed and representative state. The minority poor made up a shockingly disproportionate number of the Viet Nam dead. The draft is ended for the moment, and people are rapidly forgetting the Viet Nam period of protests and moral fulmination.

The processes by which America involved itself in that military disaster will occupy historians for years. For our purposes, a central question to be answered by future analysts is what concept of citizenship accounts for such a war, if citizenship involves representation, responsiveness, and accountability? The answer may be best understood in terms of bureaucratic constituency, clientele, and victimhood.

There was a curious and persistent discontinuity between the processes and structures of the realm of national defense and the realities of citizenship during the Viet Nam War. That war may be construed as epiphenomenal by some and as symptomatic by others. What continues to be interesting is the status of individuals and collectivities during the peace that followed. The realm of national defense appears little changed in any fundamental sense, and our relationship to it appears not to have changed.

The "curious and persistent" discontinuities between bureaucratic citizenship and patterns like MOCTI will, I believe, increase over time, in part because of the power of those who employ it and, ironically, because of the millions of citizens who condone, ignore, or are helpless to think of alternatives to it.

chapter six

The Evolving
Bureaucratic State

This final summary and conceptual chapter integrates several major concerns: the relationship between received value mixes and interaction modes; three general conceptions of public bureaucracy implied in the text; and the political power of professionalism and expertise. The chapter concludes with a brief appraisal of the book's arguments and some of the questions that arise from it.

Homo Bureaucratus Redux: Interaction Modes and Received Value Mixes

It will be recalled that received value mixes are policies embodied in the laws, rules, customs, beliefs, and desires that have regulated and directed agencies of the state and their constituent and clientele networks over time. Such mixes are political structure and serve to mark the realms of the political that I have defined simply as those places in time and space where politics takes place.

I identified three interaction modes linking persons and organizations with agencies of the state and suggested that the terms "constituent," "client," and "victim" were useful typifications of those modes. The term "mode" is to be understood both as a way of interacting and (in the statistical sense) as the most commonly appearing kind of interaction. In chapter one, it was argued that the modes were roughly

Table 6–1 Received Values That Seem to Maximize Particular Interaction Modes

Realm	Constituent			Client			Victim		
	SR	R	U	SR	R	U	SR	R	U
Political Economy									
Stimulation and Support	x			x					x
Laissez-faire individualism	x					x	x		
Regulation for expansion	x				x			x	
Intervention for system maintenance		x		x				x	
Management of complex interdependence	x			x				x	
Subtotal	8	1		4	2		2	3	
Total	9			6			5		
Social Welfare									
Institutionalization		x			x		x		
Philanthropy		x		x				x	
Moral superiority		x		x			x		
Federalization		x		x				x	
Professionalization		x		x				x	
Clientele creation		x		x			x		
Elaboration of the welfare state	x			x			x		
Subtotal	2	3		12	1		8	3	
Total	5			13			11		
National Defense									
Civilian control		x				x			x
Pax americana		x		x				x	
Science/technology as weapons	x			x					x
The garrison state	x			x			x		
Apotheosis of rationality		x			x			x	
Subtotal	4	3		6	1		2	2	
Total	7			7			4		

SR = strongly related = 2
R = related = 1
U = unrelated = 0

The greater the score, the stronger the imputed relationship between the received value mix of the realm and the indicated mode of interaction.

associated with three dimensions of interaction: the character of interest representation, efficacy (the power to alter policy outcomes), and the degree of dependency upon a public agency for the continued viability of individuals and groups.

Throughout the preceding chapters the realms of the political were seen as evolving creatures of alterations in received value mixes and were discussed in terms of these modes of interaction. In Table 6-1 I attempt to summarize graphically what I believe to be some of the connections between the eighteen values I identify with three political realms. Table 6-1 is an utterly subjective attempt at summarization and recapitulation. It is a simple matrix that reveals what I understand to be a set of interrelated phenomena.

Table 6-1 suggests that the structures produced by received value mixes tend to maximize certain kinds of interactions under particular values within given realms. For example, in the realm of political economy, stimulation and support values are identified rather strongly with constituency interaction, less strongly with client groups, and hardly at all with victimization. To demonstrate the mix of interactive modes by value and by realm, I arbitrarily quantified the strength of my conviction: values of 2, 1, or 0 are assigned to indicate that a mode is strongly related, related, or unrelated, according to relationships imputed in the text.

As indicated, the greater the score, the stronger is the imputed relationship between the received value mix of the realm and the indicated mode of interaction. By excerpting the scores aggregated from the matrix, Table 6-2 results.

This exercise in quantitative summarization suggests that in the realms discussed something resembling bureaucratic pluralism exists. By pluralism, I mean to suggest that each realm contains mixes of interactive

Table 6–2

	Interaction Mode		
Realm	Constituent	Client	Victim
Political economy	9	6	5
Social welfare	5	13	11
National defense	7	7	4
Total	21	26	20

relationships such that it is difficult to paint a given realm with the broad brush of, say, "victimization." At the same time, it seems clear that a comprehension of these realms (which make up a substantial amount of American political life) lies very much in the direction of citizenship conceived of as constituent, client, and victim. It cannot be overly stressed that I am talking about representation of interest in terms of *bureaucratic interactions* between the state and its environment.

Public Bureaucracy: Purposive Machine, Social Structure, and Political Actor

Throughout this book I have been concerned with developing a conceptual scheme that attempts to describe the roles of public bureaucracies as they have evolved within the context of American political values. I have attempted to describe the interactive nature of public bureaucracies among themselves, with other governmental institutions, and with their general environments. One clear impression should be gained from the historically descriptive exercise: *Significantly different kinds of public bureaucracies are to be found in different realms and historical periods.*

Despite this observation, I have repeatedly referred to public bureaucracy as if significant uniformities were readily observable. As in any matter of complex comparative analysis, the problem of choosing similarities and differences is central and not easily soluble. In this brief volume I have attempted to look at "boundary relationships" at the expense of comparative synthesis. In spite of this emphasis, several summary and general comparative statements can be drawn regarding the nature of public bureaucracy.

At first glance the idea of bureaucracy as a purposive machine seems to be the most uncomplicated one. Individuals join together in common cause to achieve goals attainable only through cooperative effort. Weber, Barnard, Simon, and Perrow,[1] among many others, share this essential

---

[1] Chester I. Barnard, *The Functions of the Executive* (Cambridge, Mass.: Harvard University Press, 1938); Charles Perrow, *Complex Organizations* (Glenview, Ill.: Scott, Foresman, 1972); Herbert A. Simon, *Administrative Behavior* (New York: Free Press, 1945); H. H. Gerth and C. Wright Mills, *From Max Weber* (New York: Oxford

view of formal organizations. The conception of organization as a purposive machine resting on demand and involving the aggregation of specialized tasks and resources allows one to think about public organizations *as if* they were goal-seeking mechanisms that can be designed and altered to achieve whatever purpose their creators intend.

To a remarkable extent organizations can be and are designed to function in this mechanical way. If the purposive machine metaphor works, the most successful organizations should be those involved in routinized and predictable tasks, because problems of discretion, values, and uncertainty are reduced to an absolute and tolerable minimum. The commonplace meaning of the term *bureaucracy* comes to mind with this mechanical conception. Most of us think about the routinized character of bureaucracy as being highly negative and inhumane. It is for certain kinds of problems. For most problems of mass distribution and of replicable services, however, no better system has been devised. Those who would solve the problems of the Postal Service, for instance, would improve upon precisely those mechanical aspects of bureaucracy as the term is pejoratively used.

The social order demands an efficient, effective, highly routinized and predictable purposive machine to provide the subjectively indispensable services of a postal system. No one questions these bureaucratic characteristics that demand that man–machine systems spit out predictable and cost effective results. We do not ask the Postal Service to solve social, political, ethical, or other human problems. Nor should we. Yet, at the same time we seem to demand that organizations be designed to be more humane, democratic, and responsive to their members as well as to their clients and constituents. Public bureaucracy has come to be all things to all people.

The "solution" implied in this book is that organizations in the public sector can meet the demands implied by the purposive machine metaphor only if designers look to the mixes of values in which the machines are discovered and from which they spring. The metaphor must be made more organic if one is to conceive of organizational design in an environment–man–technology–goal–impact sequence nested in a highly organized and competitive political and social order. Some recent literature in organizational design and policy analysis has begun to take this sort of

University Press, 1946); and Max Weber, *The Theory of Social and Economic Organization*, ed. Talcott Parsons (New York: Free Press, 1947).

approach, although the problems of received value mixes and political realms are not often considered.[2] A recurring problem with the purposive machine view of organization is, of course, man himself.

As complicated and ambiguous as the notion of bureaucracy as purposive machine might be, the idea of bureaucracy as social structure is even worse. This second conception of bureaucracy overlaps substantially with the first, above. If one understands that the needs, goals, and values of organization members are not coterminous with those of the organization, the problem of reconciling the two to obtain maximum productivity becomes the quintessential managerial dilemma. Ever since Taylor gave the world a view of people as malleable machines linked to real machines, the managerial problem of human social needs and organizational needs has provided a generous literature.[3] The human relations school of management argued that higher productivity could be gained by softening authoritarian and routinized hierarchical relationships, treating people like humans rather than machines, and creating environments where sociability was possible.[4] Natural adaptations to organizational formalities were found to be creative of higher productivity in many instances. All manner of employee recreational and social services were and are provided to make workers feel closer to and more at home with their organizational environment, reducing the obvious tension between their personal preferences and those embodied in organizational values. Much of this thought is directed at existing, mainly industrial, organizations. Bureaucracy as a social system might be thought of in some different lights, however.

If one steps back from the managerial perspective and looks at public organizations more generally, one can see the truth in Weber's observation about their indispensability to the social, economic, and political

[2] An outstanding example to the contrary is Garry D. Brewer, *Politicians, Bureaucrats and the Consultant* (New York: Basic Books, 1973). The impressive series edited and contributed to by Yehezkel Dror is another. See Dror's *Design for Policy Sciences* (New York: American Elsevier, 1971) and other studies in the Policy Sciences Book Series.

[3] Frederick Taylor, *Scientific Management* (New York: Harper & Row, 1947).

[4] All of this began with the Hawthorne studies (F. J. Roethlisberger and others, *Training for Human Relations* (Boston: Graduate School of Business Administration, Harvard University, 1954) and was carried forward by Chris Argyris, *Understanding Organizational Behavior* (Homewood, Ill.: Dorsey, 1960). A most interesting negative psychoanalytic statement about people in organizations is found in the application of Harry Stack Sullivan's psychological arguments. See Robert Presthus, *The Organizational Society* (New York: Vintage Books, 1962).

order. One can also see where he erred. Public organizations cannot be (and are not) uniformly monistic structures of hierarchy and specialization, as Weber suggested they were.[5] The certainties of the Postal Service simply are not discoverable in weapons procurement, drug addiction treatment, or fluctuations of the interest rate. One clear lesson that emerges from the historical narratives of the last three chapters is that *contemporary public bureaucracies are involved in nearly every problem or condition of social life and no organizational structure is appropriate to all of them.* The social structure of a problem, its environment, and the public employees charged with solving or ameliorating it vary greatly. Scientists, garbage collectors, generals, and psychiatrists cannot be structured into the same organizational forms. Thus, the social structure of task and specialization suggests a variety of organizational forms.[6]

I have implied another social structure variation which suggests another source of organizational variation. Many public bureaucracies are highly interdependent with elements of the social environment. The social structure of crime is probably as significant as the informal organizational social structure of policemen to an understanding of that realm. In the case of any social welfare or control agency, the fact that the "problems" in the environment are people suggests that the social structure of the organization may be altered thereby. Even interaction and interdependency with unorganized groups at the margins of formal organizations lead to informal adaptations on both sides. Conceiving of organization as social structure, then, involves *at least* understanding organization members as possessors of nonorganizational values, the diversity of public organizational tasks, and the interactive/interdependent influence of varying environments.[7]

I have argued that the creation of a public organization may itself be an act of political definition, since at the minimum it authoritatively identifies a problem or condition as being a matter of public concern. It was also suggested that the very structure of the organization has in some circumstances produced policy outcomes with negative consequences. In

[5] This point is most elegantly made in Victor A. Thompson, *Modern Organization* (New York: Knopf, 1964) and in his *Bureaucracy and the Modern World* (Morristown, N.J.: General Press, 1976).

[6] See James D. Thompson, *Organizations in Action* (New York: McGraw-Hill, 1967).

[7] For general theoretical statements supportive of these notions, see Bertram M. Gross, *The Managing of Organizations* (New York: Free Press, 1964) and Amitai Etzioni, *The Active Society* (New York: Free Press, 1968).

a world of perfectly linear thought, one could imagine new organizations being designed to take into account the ideas of bureaucracy as social structure, thereby creating productive entities that violate conventional norms of formal organization. One can imagine the relaxation of authority/hierarchy norms and a deemphasis of centralized control mechanisms. More organic, loosely structured, and participatory configurations for the administration of state power which are also highly flexible and adaptive to their environments are certainly within the compass of human imagination.[8] One need not have read this book to know that overarching and rigid principles of bureaucratic organization may be inappropriate, counterproductive, or dangerous to the conduct of the public business. Yet they persist.

Several interesting arguments have been made about the persistence of bureaucratic rigidities in America and in other parts of the world. These arguments center on socialization, social stratification, individual psychology, and historical determinism. This book is more narrowly focused, and no suggestion is made that these approaches to the persistence of bureaucratic social structure are necessarily contradictory. I have instead centered my attention on the political context of public bureaucracy in the American experience, and it is to this third conception that I now turn.

Public organizations are political actors because they compete and cooperate for the allocation of scarce public resources. It has been argued here that public bureaucracies take advantage of such resources as personnel, money, laws, and symbols. They also create them. People become public bureaucrats not as blank slates but as politically socialized and value laden actors who then become recipients of the values of the organization and of the received mix in which the agency is situated. To suggest that a given set of individual political values is discoverable in all bureaucrats is as dangerous as suggesting that a set of transcendent values is discoverable in all public bureaucracies.

Yet, this is a democratic society in part because of structural arrangements, but even more importantly because individuals to varying degrees carry democratic belief structures to their work. No attempt can be made here to try to assess the effect of such belief structures on the political acts of whole organizations. I raise the matter at this point simply to suggest that the macro–micro linkage between organizations and their

[8] Frank Marini (ed.), *Toward a New Public Administration* (New York: Chandler, 1971).

members has not been hypothesized as thoroughly as the linkages between bureaucracy and environment. Without speculating further, it is fair to suggest that the political beliefs of incumbent bureaucrats are significant and deserve further investigation.[9]

Another aspect of organizations as political actors that has been discussed in several contexts is the question of intrarealm constituencies or "incest groups."[10] The connection between teacher certification, education, curriculum, and the universities and state education departments is one example of this phenomenon. The movement of civilian and military officials in and out of private companies doing business with DOD is yet another example. University faculties, Wall Street law firms, and civilian appointees in the State Department constitute another incest group.

The politics and value preferences of these ascriptive groups have not been given sufficient attention in our discussion of political bureaucracy. Such groups may well be key operational actors who relate the conventional wisdom of elites to the holders of high electoral office. I suspect that the constituency politics of the realm of national defense in particular is heavily influenced by such incest groups. One mentions such relationships at the risk of overinterpretation, however, since such groups have been understood by others to be ruling elites. This understanding is at odds with the arguments presented in this book, in part because it tends to fuse the holders of wealth, high social status, and power into a series of elites who dominate all the significant realms of the political in order to further their own interests.[11]

The key political elements that I have identified rest in the general notions of professionalism, expertise, and the primacy of the state. The primacy of the state is crucial, for the state alone is that entity which can legitimately compel compliance, and bureaucratic actors are vital to an

[9] There is controversy in the literature over the operational meaning of representative bureaucracy. See Kenneth John Meier, "Representative Bureaucracy: An Empirical Analysis," *American Political Science Review* (June, 1975), 526–542 for secondary analysis of representativeness. I am unpersuaded that study of the socio-economic profile of public bureaucracy matched with that of the society tells us much about bureaucratic representation. See also Eugene B. McGregor, Jr., "Social Equity and the Public Service," *Public Administration Review* (January/February, 1974), 18–28, and Charles H. Levine, "Unrepresentative Bureaucracy—Or Knowing What You Look Like Tells Who You Are (And Maybe What To Do About It)," *The Bureaucrat* (April, 1975), 90–98.

[10] The term as far as I can tell is the creation of William J. Siffin, who used it in a public lecture at Hamilton College in 1973.

[11] C. Wright Mills, *The Power Elite* (New York: Oxford University Press, 1956).

understanding of compulsion. It may well be that political power has become diffused throughout organized society, as Wolin has suggested,[12] but those who act with the power of the state do so, I have argued, with a special symbolic power[13] that remains undiminished. The primacy of the state is evident in such realms as national defense and is less evident in realms such as political economy. When a public bureaucrat acts to affect members of society, I comprehend him to be acting with the power of the state, with all the symbolic and material meaning of that entity. When his act affects the allocation of scarce public resources, I believe him to be engaged in politics, no matter what manner of apolitical patina may be applied to his behavior.

Among the many resources employed by public bureaucracies, professionalism and expertise are particularly significant, I have suggested. When coupled with the ancient notion of the primacy of the state, they make for a formidable source of power.

This brief summary of three conceptions of public organizations devolves now to the isolation and analysis of the question of public bureaucratic professionalism and expertise in terms of the policy process.

The Political Power of Professionalism and Expertise

In 1960, if one excluded political appointees and the thousands of persons indirectly employed by the state through contracts, subsidies, and grants, nearly one-third of all public employees were in professional and technical occupational categories. According to Frederick Mosher, this was more than three times the comparable proportion in the private sector. My guess is that examination of more recent data, particularly in state and local governments, would now reveal an even greater proportion. Mosher provides a list of interdependencies between government and profession which summarizes many of the examples discussed in the previous three chapters. Although my approach and conclusions differ from Mosher's, much summary overlap can be seen in the following:[14]

[12] Sheldon S. Wolin, *Politics and Vision* (Boston: Little, Brown, 1960), Chapter 10, "The Age of Organization and the Sublimation of Politics."

[13] Murray Edelman, *The Symbolic Uses of Politics* (Urbana: University of Illinois Press, 1970).

[14] Frederick C. Mosher, *Democracy and the Public Service* (New York: Oxford University Press, 1968), pp. 103–104.

Governments are, or have been:

> *The creators of many professions.*
> *The legitimizers of all those which have been legitimized.*
> *Protectors of the autonomy, integrity, monopoly, and standards of those who have such protections.*
> *The principal supporters of their research and of that of the sciences upon which they depend.*
> *Subsidizers of much of their education.*
> *Among their principal employers and the nearly exclusive employers of some of them, which means also*
> *Among the principal users of their knowledge and skills.*

For their part, the professions:

> *Contribute to government a very substantial proportion of public servants.*
> *Provide much of the leadership in a considerable number of public agencies.*
> *Through their educational programs, examinations, accreditation, and licensing, very largely determine what the content of each profession is in terms of knowledge, skills, and work.*
> *Influence public policy and the definition of public purpose in those many fields within which they operate.*
> *In varying degree and in different ways provide or control the recruitment, selection, and other personnel actions for their members.*
> *Shape the structure as well as the social organization of many public agencies.*

That professionals are present in government in large and significant numbers and that they have grown in importance over time is hardly at issue. The question is, are they as politically significant as I have claimed? If they are significant politically, how and why has this come to pass? What are the causal factors and mechanisms for their claimed centrality in the policy process? I shall deal with the last two questions in the hope that doing so will make a positive case for the first.

It has been argued here that the realms of the political are places in time and space defined by received value mixes that are reflective of enduring policies. This line of reasoning permits the inclusion of value change through a variety of mechanisms, one of which involves structural changes in the social order. In each realm one can see professionalism and expertise emerging over time; they take many forms and have different meanings and impact because of the distinct historical forces that have shaped the different realms.

The evolving dominance of professionalism has come to pass for several reasons, the most important of which can be traced to structural alterations in the social order. Weber tells us about subjective indispensability, and I have discussed the conversion of wants into needs.[15] If one believes the argument that there is growing interdependence throughout the social order and that people have *ever elaborating needs* for more and better services which are *compounded by the wants of relative deprivation,* then a source for the growing domination of professionalism and expertise in general is clear. Within the general society, vital services have become the monopoly of professionals and experts.

This has come about because we believe that we cannot live without certain professional services, and we do not wish to live without others. Furthermore, the culture contains a powerful belief in the value of detached knowledge, said to be possessed by professionals and experts. Whether such belief is justified in all professions or whether all people believe it uniformly is beside the point. In general, we have seen the fruits of profession and expertise and we have found them useful.

In addition, those who provide services are commonly awarded social deference and material reward. As we have valued science, technology, and their successful products, so, too, have we valued the processes and assumptions that create them. Thus, one can perceive admiration, respect, and even fear of the mysteries of professionalized and expert service creation and provision. Utilitarian and affective characteristics of professionalism and expertise are highly, if not uniformly, valued in the general society. More specifically, those who are themselves professionally trained or highly educated are likely to value the attributes of professionalism and expertise. It is also true that those who participate in and influence politics now tend to be among the better educated of society.

Slowly at first and then with increasing velocity, the realms of the political began to reflect these structural changes in the social order. I have traced patterns of increasing specialization of tasks and persons in three political realms. Early in this century the belief systems of the educated began to be noticeable as their values became structural entities such as the city manager system, the public health service, and the grow-

[15] Chapter 2, pp. 47–52.

ing civilian employment of the Army Corps of Engineers. Because politics was and to a great extent still is a dirty word in America, many sincere, enlightened politicians and ordinary citizens believe(d) that the introduction of professionals and professionalized knowledge would improve and change the nature of politics itself. The ideals of neutral competence and objective sources of knowledge in the formulation of public policy are probably as significant in modern American political culture as the ideals of freedom of expression and representative democracy.

From an analytical perspective, the problem is that we fail to have a theory of the state that encompasses representative democracy and a highly professionalized bureaucracy. The clichés and distinctions that once attempted to reconcile the two are in trouble today. The politics/administration dichotomy of Max Weber and Woodrow Wilson simply does not work.[16] The separation of powers doctrine, so dear to the heart of American democratic ideology, is also in some difficulty. The public/private distinction has been dealt a series of blows in the political and scholarly worlds.[17]

A variety of historical pressures have tended to alter, if not destroy, these hoary notions of American government. Some of these pressures have been identified in the preceding chapters and discussed at considerable length. At the risk of excessive repetition and overgeneralization, I continue the discussion of professionalism and expertise in an attempt to formulate a broader conception of the policy process. This partially answers the question of the mechanisms for the claimed centrality of professionalized bureaucrats in the policy process. I hope thereby to illuminate the continuing dilemmas of the politics/administration dichotomy and the separation of powers doctrine.

If one accepts the structural change in the social order hypothesis above, and the subjective indispensability notion reformulated from Weber, then the mechanisms of power employed by political bureaucracy are very important. One must begin macroscopically and note two significant observations made by Herbert Simon, among others. If one were to imagine the entire political system, including citizens, clients, constituents, and victims, as a policy-formulating structure, what would be some

---

[16] See Dwight Waldo, *The Administrative State* (New York: Ronald Press, 1948) and Vincent Ostrom, *The Intellectual Crisis in American Public Administration* (Alabama: University of Alabama Press, 1973).

[17] Theodore J. Lowi, *The End of Liberalism* (New York: Norton, 1969) and Grant McConnell, *Private Power and American Democracy* (New York: Knopf, 1967).

of its major characteristics? Simon points us first to the question of attention as a scarce resource.[18]

If great numbers of nonbureaucratic political actors concentrated their energies on a single issue or set of issues, then the power of professionalized bureaucrats would, in my view, be diminished. The normal situation is the opposite: Attention to single issues by large numbers of people in the political system is an extraordinary event.[19] Because of the diversity and complexity of important matters, discrete publics tend to focus attention very briefly on any single matter. Robert Dahl and other pluralist writers have made this point well.[20] Those who dispute the conclusions of the pluralists have drawn from Schattschneider and pointed to the "nondecisions" of major importance which never become issues.[21]

One can further argue about why some issues get raised and others do not. The point is that attention to a given problem is scarce in the general political system, and prolonged attention is extremely rare. Certainly, it is true that Congress possesses considerable potential power over the policy process, but its ability to be attentive to all issues is severely constrained. Congressmen and senators have limited attentive capacities because of the range and complexity of issues on their personal and institutional agendas. Attention to issues, then, is a scarce resource in nearly every entity of political structure from persons to political systems.

A second observation is that attention is also serial. Even those citizens and congressmen who do maintain a high level of interest in a given issue area discover that a specific problem must be dropped temporarily when another arises. Thus, if one wants to be attentive to the problems of public education in America, one must first narrow the range of issues considered and then must order the sequence of their consideration. If new issues arise (or are discovered), old ones must be set aside. If one gets into the matter of curriculum, for instance, then the significant tangential questions of personnel, training, and finance arise and may require consideration before returning to the initial matter of concern.

[18] Herbert A. Simon, "The Changing Theory and Changing Practice of Public Administration," in Joseph A. Uveges, Jr., *The Dimensions of Public Administration,* 2nd ed. (Boston: Holbrook Press, 1975), pp. 28–53.

[19] Donald J. Devine, *The Attentive Public: Polyarchical Democracy* (Chicago: Rand McNally, 1970).

[20] Robert A. Dahl, *Who Governs?* (New Haven: Yale University Press, 1961).

[21] Peter Bachrach and Morton S. Baratz, *Power and Poverty* (New York: Oxford University Press, 1970).

These observations are probably correct at any level of analysis in the political world, but they are particularly interesting in the context of political bureaucracy. While the structure of bureaucratic organization can be partially understood in terms of the division of a problem into its simplest elements, the matters of attention and seriality do not disappear: They are simply reduced by the fact of specialization of persons and of tasks. Bureaucrats concerned with financing public education are themselves divided into a series of prolonged attention subsystems. Those concerned with the issuance and redemption of bonds are not necessarily closely related to those who have operating responsibility for the annual budget.

Yet, if we were to locate a single spot within the political system where knowledgeability and prolonged attention are most in evidence, it would probably be with the professionalized bureaucrats. It is from them that data flows describing problems. The division of labor is also the division of attention. Although attention is serial for bureaucrats as well as for congressmen, the range of serial considerations is much narrower in the former case. Most certainly this is truer still for the general public. Electoral politicians following vote maximization strategies[22] at the national or state level are often in the uncomfortable position of having to avoid issue stances that might alienate some possible supporters. They often are forced to manufacture issues to appear "issue-oriented" and to avoid reducing their options if elected.

This is not to suggest that once elected, chief executives and legislators lack power and influence. Rather, their capacity to alter policy outcomes is mitigated by the scarcity of their attentiveness to any given policy issue and by the necessarily serial nature of their consideration. They are further hampered in their capacity to make decisions by a set of factors inherent to professionalized bureaucracy. These factors center around the complex division of specialized knowledge into enduring patterns of bureaucratic institutionalization.

Professional bureaucrats dominate those vast segments of the policy process that do not become major issues. In other words, if the "scope of conflict"[23] does not involve large numbers of powerful actors or if no real conflict takes place at all, I argue that bureaucratic initiative, innovation, or inertia will prevail. This can be interpreted to mean that

[22] Anthony Downs, *An Economic Theory of Democracy* (New York: Harper & Row, 1957).

[23] E. E. Schattschneider, *The Semi-Sovereign People* (New York: Holt, 1960).

bureaucrats deal only with noncontroversial matters, defined as simply unimportant. Alternatively, it could be argued that the important noncontroversial matters with which bureaucrats deal are not issues simply because widespread consensus exists concerning them.

This book specifically rejects both arguments. If one were to consider the resources devoted to national defense, for example, and were to look at the annual appropriations for DOD, one might conclude that here is an area of widespread consensus in which bureaucrats act simply as functionaries. The Defense Department obtained an average 90 percent plus of their budget requests over a twenty-year period, suggesting that controversy occurred only at the margins and that 90 percent of what DOD did during the period 1954–1974 was therefore either unimportant or not controversial. The discussion and analysis in the previous chapter as well as any reading of contemporary history suggest rather strongly that what DOD did (as symbolized by the legitimating process of congressional acquiescence to budgetary requests) *was* terribly significant. Many activities of that vast bureaucracy were noncontroversial only because they never reached a point where those capable of effectively disagreeing could make their voices heard.

This sort of thing comes about because of secrecy, scarcity, and seriality of attention, and because of bureaucrats' power to overwhelm laymen with expertise. The latter is particularly significant in my view (although not in Simon's).[24] It has been my observation that in every realm discussed one can discover the capacity of political actors to defer to vocabularies and esoterica they cannot learn or fathom easily. In realms where powerful and organized actors can mobilize themselves into constituent relationships, mutual co-option and incest groups predominate. Thus, there is a sharing of professionalized knowledge among powerful economic actors inside and outside government which serves to bring closure to issues within specific elements of the realm of political economy. The relationships between the major banks and those who regulate them typify the power of such professionalized knowledge. This example also extends to such areas as agricultural policies and defense procurement activities.

In realms where client and victim relationships predominate, the power of professionalized knowledge has been illustrated in a number of

[24] Simon, "The Changing Theory and Changing Practice of Public Administration."

settings. An otherwise educated person who is outside the professional-ized education incest group faces a real dilemma when confronted by the jargon of those who dominate that realm. Medical and psychiatric areas are similar in the impenetrability of their language. One has difficulty knowing what they are doing without first understanding the terms pro-fessionals use in describing their actions. Certainly, less well-educated clients and victims are at an even greater disadvantage. But the posses-sion of esoteric knowledge (which in many cases is necessarily obfus-cated by jargon) is only one source of professional bureaucratic power. The information contained in that knowledge and how it is used are even more significant.

Traditional thought on the policy process suggests that the initiation of a program or policy is a political act and its administration is a bureau-cratic function. In general, I have suggested that a different process occurs. Professional bureaucrats are charged with responsibility for gen-erating relevant data and communicating it in the policy process. This responsibility has both organizational and professional roots. While infor-mation may be true or false, it is seldom neutral. Which data are col-lected to serve what ends is a valuative matter that lies deep in the professional and organizational roots of the data gatherers, synthesizers, and communicators. Professionals are structured into hierarchical rela-tionships within bureaucratic structures. Information about significant changes in the environment or in mechanical and organizational technol-ogies generally must *move up* through a structure of authority and defer-ence. Therefore, what is communicated to whom and in what sequence are of great moment to the study of any policy.

Bureaucrats, like the rest of us, are value-laden creatures. Values that help us to perceive, order, and restructure reality are by definition fundamental in any form of social behavior. Professionals, by definition, come to the bureaucratic enterprise with sets of standards of ethical practice and conventional wisdom that are products of their occupational training. They meet and adapt to the organizational and general received values of the formal role they fill in public service. The kinds of data, problems, and possible solutions perceived as significant through the valuative lenses of profession, formal role, and received mix define the range of premises which they are able to see and communicate. Premise creation is a complex matter at both the individual and group levels and deserves much more attention than can be given here. It suffices at this point to suggest that the premises created by professionalized bureaucrats differ from and overlap with those of electoral politicians and bureaucratic constituents.

At the risk of overgeneralization, one professional premise that might be loosely posited as an overarching value is the commitment to initiate and innovate. The values of initiation and innovation, like any values, are not uniformly diffused through all professions, and they are almost always part of a contradictory received mix. Yet, professionalized bureaucracy has the talents, resources, and motivations to alter the existing state of affairs to its own benefit and to the benefit of the social order. Bureaucrats control the gathering, transmission, and interpretation of data. They exist in political and social realms that are habituated to technological change as a major source of social, political, and economic benefit, no matter the negative consequences of some past performances. Simon summarizes the argument nicely:[25]

. . . *For the professional, activities contributing to relevant values are always high on the agenda. The professional has a stake in innovations in his specialty that gives them claim on his attention. Second, the professional attends to the parts of his environment from which innovations may emerge that can be adopted or adapted; he is a principal channel of cultural diffusion within his specialty from other jurisdictions and from the sources of new research and development. Third, the professional wants the esteem of fellow professionals—hence he is motivated to innovate for their approval. Fourth, the professional has the technical knowledge and skill that enable him to devise, recognize, adapt, and evaluate potential innovations.*

. . . *In a highly technical society, and particularly one that is receptive to innovation, the technicians will be a main source of innovation—and for government this means the bureaucracy and associated professions and often the two of them in concert. The "power" to innovate—even subject to political approval—does not fit the classical categories of power and influence, but is power nonetheless. It is probably the principal power of the bureaucracy in the realm of policy and value.*

Simon's statement is reflective of a general premise discoverable within the received value mix of professionals in public bureaucracy. There are, I have suggested, equally powerful values that minimize and reduce the impact of initiation and innovation. Inertia, stasis, and a com-

[25] Ibid., p. 48.

mitment to the status quo are probably more characteristic of public bureaucracy than are initiation and innovation. Once again, the analysis is confronted with an inherent contradiction in a value mix, this time in values said to apply in many realms.

Those aspects of bureaucratic life that tend to regard precedent as writ coexist with innovational properties. While I do not believe that one can explain away the conflict, it is made more understandable by suggesting that some structures of bureaucratic power more than others in any given realm are devoted to innovation. In general, the police are involved primarily in system maintenance while R&D bureaucracies clearly are in the innovation business.

The matter of initiative is a somewhat different problem from innovation. Initiation of policy alternatives from bureaucratic sources is a highly politicized process involving careful intrarealm negotiations and conflict. To alter existing policy through administrative rulemaking is often a significant initiative step and usually requires constituency approval or acquiescence. Initiatives that require congressional approval involve behaviors that I have identified as explicitly political, since they often involve shifts in the extant allocative pattern. Most initiation from the bureaucracy is not controversial, although it may be important. Change in the existing pattern of allocation of resources is normally incremental[26] and is partially a function of alterations in the environment of the realm. The power of innovation is more a function of profession than is the power of initiation which is highly associated with the clout possessed by the managerial elites dominating bureaucratic structure. The nontechnical managers of public bureaucracy, generalist professionals, often *select* from among innovations those which will redound to the benefit of the organization. Similarly, they may reject useful innovations that they perceive to be injurious to the organization. The resistance to aircraft as a military weapon, despite its demonstrated effectiveness in World War I, is an example of the difference between the power to innovate and the power to initiate. The capacity to destroy new ideas is as great as the capacity to create them, because bureaucracies are, above all, structures of power, control, and routine, created in part by value mixes received from the past.

[26] Two classics provide explanations for this phenomenon at individual and collective levels: Charles E. Lindblom, "The Science of 'Muddling Through,'" *Public Administration Review* (1959), 79–88 and Aaron Wildavsky, *The Politics of the Budgetary Process*, 2nd ed. (Boston: Little, Brown, 1964).

A final mechanism of professional bureaucratic power remains to be discussed. One of the dominant attributes of professionalism is its predictability. Professionals by definition are committed to standards of behavior in the conduct of their official duties upon which politicians can rely. One reasonably expects government lawyers, doctors, social workers, and the like to perform their functions in conformity with their professional credos. This predictability involves detachment and neutrality in the discretionary aspects of professional routines. The greatest source of direction and control is therefore made available to the political system by the fact that these important actors have *internalized* a set of predictable, valuative behaviors. Such people require little direct supervision of their behavior in the conventional hierarchical sense. The predictability of professionals is a great source of power and influence, since it smacks of the neutral competence and removal from politics so valued in many realms.

A problematic situation arises when one comes to deal with the incommensurability of values found among professionals. It is one thing to rejoice in the neutral competence of social workers, but quite a different matter when one must confront the question of need. A social worker may be relied upon to deal with a client according to the approved norms of his profession, but he cannot tell me how many social workers there *ought to be.* Detachment disappears when the question of allocating scarce public resources arises. The professional becomes a significant political actor when he claims that more resources are needed to improve or expand services, for he thereby mixes his professional status with the business of resource allocation.

All the status and deference powers of expert knowledge are brought to bear in this kind of politics. One thinks of Admiral Rickover, Robert Moses, J. Edgar Hoover, and Wernher von Braun representing their professional values in the service of the explicitly political problem of allocating scarce public resources. While each may have been neutrally competent and respected as a professional, each managed to trade on that respected professionalism in order to gain control over resources. Such behavior would not be possible if those in the political system (but outside the bureaucracy) were not so convinced of the legitimacy of professionals as advocates.

Traditional ideas about the policy process would have us believe that the incommensurability of values in political life in general is resolved through bargaining and negotiation in the formally political branches of government. This is not always the case, however, because professionals not only convert the respect for their professions to political advantage, but they also dominate the perceptions of the possible. They accomplish this by creating and manipulating the data upon which alternatives and premises rest. The American political system has no theory that accurately accounts for the problem of the incommensurability of professional values and the political advocacy of professionals.

I have suggested five mechanisms and factors that enhance the power of professionalized bureaucrats in the policy process. Their summarization and recapitulation lead to some final questions about the future of the American political system. I have argued that:

1. Change in the social order and in the political system in general has brought about a heightened legitimacy for those who profess neutral competence and detached behaviors in the discovery of new knowledge and in the conduct of the public business.

2. The scarcity of attention and the serial nature of problem or issue consideration in the whole political system tend to favor the "prolonged attention subsystems" of professionalized bureaucrats. Many matters, important and unimportant, never become part of an expanded zone of conflict because of the domination and partition of policy areas into realms dominated by relatively small "incest" and constituency groups. In realms characterized mainly by client and victim interaction modes, issues are most likely to arise out of intrarealm or interrealm conflict.

3. Specialized knowledge and professional norms encouraging innovation and discovery, coupled with the "prolonged attention span" of bureaucracy, give professionalized public bureaucrats a capacity to initiate and innovate which is unexcelled in the political system.

4. Professionalized bureaucrats dominate information creation, analysis, and transmission, thereby giving them a capacity to structure and suppress alternatives and premises. The alternatives from which political actors select are nearly always created by professionalized bureaucrats who naturally build into the alternatives sets of premises that are seldom in conflict with their professional and organizational values. This process and the power inherent in routine and precedent account for much of the inertia and stasis that counter initiative and innovation.

5. There is an incommensurability of professional and allocative values that is bridged by attempting to ignore the difference between the

two. Most politicians and bureaucrats tend to ignore the gap between an actor who is at once a claimant on scarce public resources and an expert in the policy area for which he claims need.

This discussion of professionalism and expertise in public bureaucracy is intended to be summary but not conclusive. I believe that each of the five factors and mechanisms is readily discoverable in the analysis of the three political realms discussed. Furthermore, I think that the five general properties summarized above when combined with the power inherent in the bureaucratic interaction modes analyzed earlier yield the outline of an evolving and emerging bureaucratic state.

The Bureaucratic State: Nobody Runs Everything (But Sometimes Somebody Runs Something)

When a book or a course comes to an end, there is a tendency to want the author or instructor to supply either the end, the answer, or the truth. This is so not only because people are tidy, but because much of our thought is linear: If things don't have a beginning, middle, and end, then they at least ought to supply an answer. Social scientists and college professors in general are notorious for their capacities to be inconclusive and to answer questions with other questions. Knowing some truth is, of course, unsatisfyingly short of knowing *the* truth. This book is an attempt to describe some aspects of complex political and social reality. It is discontinuous and has no convenient end, in part because of the author's failure, but also because public bureaucracy is itself inherently contradictory. With these caveats and disclaimers in mind, I conclude with some typically unsatisfyingly incomplete observations and questions about the evolving bureaucratic state.

I began by noting that people interact with their government mainly through organizations or in organizationally defined settings. Citizenship, I argued, was really comprehensible in one's life in terms of bureaucratic constituency, clientele, or victim modes of interaction. This argument led to devising a conceptual scheme that would deal with two kinds of questions. The first of these derived from the initial observations of chapter one and can be stated thus: If it is true that we are a nation of bureaucratic constituents, clients, and victims, then what conception of politics and of the political system explains that fact? Second, how has it all come to pass?

My attempts to answer these large questions are encompassed in the conceptual scheme of Chapter two and in the illustrative historical analysis of the three realms of the political that follow. In pursuit of the argument, I have clearly avoided important matters which seemed beside the point and some which were not. The most serious of the latter are questions about the internal workings and characteristics of political bureaucracies, a matter that deserves at least another volume. In order to pursue my major themes I have also understated the significance of the relationships of public bureaucracies to legislatures, elected executives, and courts. Given these and other limitations, what conclusions might be drawn about the nature of the American political system and its future?

Structures of participation inherited from the past are either dead or transformed. Much of what passes for political participation in the American electoral arena is not much more than dramaturgy and symbolism, removed from issues and policies. The citizenry can be roused to diffuse anger and protests which are sometimes converted to policy response, but this is a rare occurrence. The Viet Nam War dragged on through several political campaigns before a combination of enemy action, ally incompetence, and elected politicians' fear of ultimate retribution at the polls finally brought the war to a close. An enduring issue of modern domestic politics crops up again in the busing issue. Like the Viet Nam War, one can see signs of widespread civil disobedience developing in response to policies in which the citizens of the nation did not participate. They are like the war protesters, clients or victims, perhaps even like constituents, but they are not citizens in the classical tradition of the history books. I have attempted to show how and why this is so. I have also tried to suggest that there are dozens of matters of potential importance to nearly the entire polity that never get on anyone's agenda and never will. I believe that the number of such matters is increasing.

The scale and complexity of modern government and of the problems with which it is supposed to deal make the ideal of representative democracy problematic, if not impossible. No one person or group of persons runs the government. No one runs the Defense Department. One searches with difficulty for those accountable for policy outcomes, even in general areas like public welfare, and then discovers that the unit of analysis is too broad. The vision of investigators must narrow within the realm to its elements in order even to begin the job of discovering who governs.

This process of narrowing the scope of analysis reflects a political and philosophical reality: *A theory of politics that implies that somebody or some set of institutions runs everything cannot be sustained.* Balance wheel notions of federalism and separation of powers are less applicable today than ever before. Elite and other deterministic arguments are similarly difficult to sustain. I have suggested that a general phenomenon, government by bureaus, is highly significant to any explanation of policy. I have not argued that bureaucrats run everything, but that public bureaucracy as a general concept is increasingly central to an understanding of all political phenomena.

The power and primacy of the state are diffused among a variety of actors in public and private organizational settings such that it is difficult to articulate a single explanatory theory of American politics. The key elements of representation and accountability through political control by electorates are absent in most realms of the political. What one can see is the monopoly over compliance rules diffused well beyond the legal and conceptual boundaries of the past. Managerial power is exercised within the realms of the political. But to manage is not to govern.

To argue that one can discover no single set of actors dominating the powers of the state is not to suggest that political power is not being exercised. On the contrary, I believe that I have identified, described, and analyzed enormous concentrations of political power within the corpus of what I have loosely called the state. These concentrations of power appear so discontinuous that it hardly makes sense to talk about the realm of social welfare and control and its integration with the realm of national defense. I also believe that no politician integrates them, nor do many constituents and clients; certainly, not many victims do.

Yet, one wishes to discover an integrating rule or principle, not only because of a desire to know "the end, the answer, or the truth." One must attempt the task of integration at any level for two fundamental reasons. Political bureaucracy in America is the single most powerful conceptual and political entity, in my view. If I am even partially correct, then citizens must attempt to gain as much control over these structures as possible to avoid at least some of the more unpleasant aspects of the structures' actions. The polity helped to create political bureaucracy and it sustains it. The fundamental question of the citizenry's control over its government has shifted since the eighteenth century from legislatures and parties to new and much more complicated terrain. The first and most fundamental question is *what do we mean by representative bureaucracy and how can we achieve it so that the interests of citizens are authoritatively taken into account in the formation of public policy?*

Public interest lobbies and various sections of social welfare, housing, and planning legislation have all contributed to attempts at community participation. The co-optive powers of bureaucratic agencies and the relative weakness of their clients lead me to be suspicious of such approaches. I do not foresee the ready conversion of clients into constituents through a wave of the legislative or bureaucratic wand. The differing interaction modes did not come about because of some design, but because powerful actors inside and outside the apparatus of the state created them in the context of a set of received values. Nor do I see powerful actors striving toward increased bureaucratic representativeness and accountability, particularly in such realms as national defense.

As significant as are the questions surrounding the basic democratic values of representativeness and accountability in bureaucratic settings, a related question seems equally fundamental. If it is true that daily we become more interdependent with complex public and private systems over which we have little understanding and less control, then what is the general drift of the social order? I have argued that government is central to the conduct of our lives, whether we like it or not. I have suggested that there is a range of dependencies that differs according to one's socio-economic status, group membership, and where one is in the cycle of one's life. If one accepts the centrality of complex systems of political power in the partial determination of the future, then *to what ends are those complex systems to be managed, if indeed they can be managed at all?*

Are complex mechanical and organizational technologies so thoroughly embedded that they have in effect become autonomous, especially in the unanticipated consequences of their interaction? The most ancient questions of government revolved around valuative choice, such that powerful actors through one means or another were able to alter and control actions of the state according to their visions of self-interest or altruistic truths. The point is, *they* chose. Can contemporary political actors choose among values which defy, alter, or manage the logics of the complex interdependent technological systems? One most decidedly hopes so, yet the assessment of some of our history contained in this book does not offer much positive evidence. The management of complex interdependence is the politics of the future, I believe, yet we have precious little to guide us in that task. The embryonic efforts at analysis, description, and control do not logically lead to a valuative idea of political management. Such an idea (or more accurately ideas) would not only provide a view of preferable end-states, but would provide the costs and transformation rules for their achievement.

If one were to connect the two questions and restate them, one might create the question: How are we to govern democratically that which we so imperfectly understand? I cannot answer the question. I hope to have illuminated what I believe to be the systemic drift which is in effect an answer, albeit an unhappy and imperfect one. A nation of constituents, clients, and victims is not likely to create broad valuative ends for the future or the transformation rules to achieve them.

Nor is a nation of essentially uncoordinated but interactive political realms dominated by bureaucrats likely to provide such broad valuative ends. One might speculate about the future of the bureaucratic state in any number of ways. One speculation in particular strikes me as interesting, since it combines some aspects of two or more received values into a political mechanism that might provide a set of circumstances beneficially disruptive of public bureaucratic power.

If one assumes that professionalism, differentially valued and powerful in several realms, is a growing feature of public bureaucracy and of the social order in general, then it may have reached the status of a *systemically general* received value. If this is the case (and I believe it is imminent), then the problem of countering the power of professionalized bureaucrats may become an aspect of American political structure. This could happen in the following way: The norms that permit legitimated dissent within a profession may be combined with the ancient democratic value of "the loyal opposition" to create structures of political debate that would focus on bureaucratic policymaking.

Opposition legitimated by professional status and by the received values of honest dissent and loyal opposition might become institutionalized in interesting ways as America and its public agencies become more professionalized. Dissident experts organizing themselves around issues or issue clusters *central to their expertise* may be a source of policy alternatives in the future bureaucratic state. Nobel prize winners in biology who make proclamations about public welfare or morality are not what I have in mind, for such activities vitiate the power such persons hold professionally. The same actors speaking on genetic research *over time and within an organizational setting* could be a very potent force, if I am correct about the strength with which Americans inside public bureaucracies and in the general political system value professionalized expertise.

This speculation forces one to imagine sets of dissident professionals tolerated and respected by their dominant peers in public bureaucracy. It further requires one to imagine that such professionals are organized and actively seek coalition with other political actors in order to achieve commonly shared end-states. One can then speculate about the possibility of a more highly educated public becoming involved as issues develop which are salient to them and about which they are somewhat knowledgeable. Similar involvements with legislators might also be assumed.

What might such assumptions combine to become in the way of an imagined political structure? Professionals organized as dissidents, loyally opposed to the policies of incumbent bureaucratic experts and allied with other political actors, could lead to a structure of representation that would partially alleviate some of the negative aspects of bureaucratic citizenship. Issue-specific expertise plus the skills of bureaucratic politics and a familiarity with the ways of political power are increasingly being disseminated throughout the populations of certain professions. The political naiveté of physical scientists has been reduced substantially in the past generation. I suspect that city planners, social workers, educationists, and others are learning the skills of politics and bureaucratic power such that the possibility of dissent that endures over time and that is organized and professionally legitimated exists.

I believe that such professionalized political ferment exists within each realm of the political today and that it might lead to the development of professionally and politically legitimated loyal oppositions to incumbent bureaucratic power. In some ways, the received values of legislative lobbying, obligatory professional dissent over technical matters, the ideas of bureaucratic constituency and loyal opposition might be blended to yield a new set of structures in the evolving policy processes.

Such speculation is easily overstated. Some professions by virtue of their history and social structure are more likely to adapt to modern conditions of public bureaucratic power than are others. Professional military officers, geneticists, and social workers have profoundly different histories regarding public political dissent, and one would be foolish to speculate that those historical value foundations would crumble. In some areas, however, there is an overlap between the obligation to dissent on technical questions and very important matters of public policy. The most obvious cases of such overlap occur in the physical, natural, and social sciences.

Perhaps in some of these professions the germs of an alteration in the received value mixes of some of the realms of the political might take place, as I have outlined above. It might be that public bureaucracy itself contains some complementary germs of internal dissent among professionals. A coalition of such elements plus some other political actors might be powerful enough to develop some opposition networks. Such configurations of issue-centered power could at least form the basis for a challenge to the growing dominance of professionalized political power in the bureaucratic state.

Index